Staying Close to the River

Other Books by Ken Worpole

Republic of Letters, edited with Dave Morley (1982)

Dockers and Detectives (1983)

Reading By Numbers (1984)

Death in the City, with Melissa Benn (1986)

Saturday Night or Sunday Morning? From Arts to Industry – New Forms of Cultural Policy, with Geoff Mulgan (1986)

City Centres, City Cultures, with Mark Fisher MP (1988)

Towns for People: New Issues in Urban Policy (1992)

Libraries in an Era of Cultural Change, with Liz Greenhalgh and Charles Landry (1995)

Staying Close to the River:

Reflections on Travel and Politics

Ken Worpole

Lawrence & Wishart Ltd
144a Old South Lambeth Road
London Sw8 1XX

First published 1995
by Lawrence & Wishart

0 85315 820 7

Photoset by Action Typesetting Ltd, Gloucester

Printed and bound in Great Britain by
Redwood Books, Trowbridge.

For Larraine, Ben & Anna

With love and affection, as always

Many people have been involved directly and indirectly in this book over the years, and therefore it would seem insidious to try to count or name them. However, three people must be named: Dave Morley, Rebecca O'Rourke and Jenny Uglow. It was their advice and editing skills which brought this book to fruition. I also owe a particular debt of thanks to Ruth Borthwick at Lawrence & Wishart, whose enthusiasm for the project finally made it happen.

As a life's work, I would remember everything – everything, against loss. I would go through life like a plankton net. I would trap and keep every teacher's funny remark, every face on the street, every microscopic alga's sway, every conversation, configuration of leaves, every dream, and every scrap of overhead cloud...Some days I felt an urgent responsibility to each change of light outside the sunporch windows. Who would remember any of it, any of this our time, and the wind thrashing the buckeye limbs outside? Somebody had to do it, somebody had to hang on to the days with teeth and fists, or the whole show had been in vain.

Annie Dillard, *An American Childhood,* 1988

Your letters contain nothing but nothing except for The Worker's Cause...When I open your letters and see six sheets covered with debates about the Polish Socialist Party, and not a single word about ordinary life, I feel faint.

Rosa Luxemburg's Letters to Leo Jogiches, edited and translated by Elzbieta Ettinger, 1981

'The wistful though firm resolution of the exiles of yesterday can teach us to live correctly under today's conditions. To be orphaned by ideologies is natural, as it is natural to lose one's own parents. It is a grievous moment, but not one that induces us to profane our lost fathers, because it does not mean abandoning what has been taught us.

Claude Magris, *Danube,* 1986

But if we could ever become reconciled to the idea that most of reality is indifferent to our descriptions of it, and that the human self is created by the use of a vocabulary rather than being adequately or inadequately expressed in a vocabulary, then we should at last have assimilated what was true in the Romantic idea that truth is made rather than found.

Richard Rorty, *Contingency, Irony and Solidarity,* 1988

Contents

Introduction

The letters which follow are real letters, selected from a number sent over recent years to friends, mostly posted from the same letter box that stands by the gates of Clissold Park, close to where I have lived for the past twenty-five years. When I started writing them it never occurred to me that one day, partly urged on by friends, partly because I am by nature a documentarist, some of them might be published.

I started to write letters when the certainties of political change began to fall apart, and when doubt and a degree of detachment replaced enthusiasm for change at all costs. Often, late at night, I would sit down when the house was quiet and try to share with friends some of the doubts and difficulties that seemed to bedevil the projects we were engaged in, on all sides. Writing seemed to be a way of holding on, at least to all the valuable and worthwhile experiences, ideas and relationships that had been lived through in the years of political activism and certainty. Salman Rushdie has written eloquently about this: 'Never forget that writing is as close as we get to keeping a hold on the thousand and one things – childhood, certainties, cities, doubts, dreams, instants, phrases, parents, loves – that go on slipping, like sand, through our fingers.'[1] The Danish writer, Suzanne Brøgger, says that writing allows us to step into the same river twice.

For me writing has been indissolubly linked with politics. At an impressionable and intense age – a working-class pupil at a snobbish, authoritarian and benighted grammar school – I chanced upon, and became totally caught up in, a heady local sub-culture of beatnik poetry, modern jazz and revolutionary politics, a roller-coaster ride through a welter of ideas, books, debates, meetings and demonstrations, that was wholly exhilarating and self-affirming until, many years later, I fell to earth. Yet I still feel emotionally and intellectually attached to those formative years. The banner of many in this period was inscribed with Marx's dictum that hitherto the philosophers have merely sought to interpret the world, the point was to change it. Action preceded thought and understanding, and sometimes dispensed with the latter stages

1 Introduction to *Günter Grass: On Writing and Politics,* Penguin, Harmondsworth, 1987.

altogether. Today, while I still want to see the world changed, I also want to understand it too.

Writing is a pre-eminent way of understanding. The long pause and the wrestling with words between the thought and the tentative pressing of the typewriter keys, is the moment when simplicity and certainty is exchanged for complexity and doubt. Speech may be wittier, but writing is usually wiser. A long gaze out of the window between sentences invariably helps. A taxi-driver friend of mine, another assiduous keeper of notebooks and diaries, tells me that whenever he is unaccountably shocked or disturbed by an incident in the course of his work – the mugging and slashing of an old woman, a knife fight outside a club, the rape of a prostitute – he comes to terms with his depression by writing it all down. Understanding helps anneal the pain.

When I first started writing some thirty years ago, there were a limited number of literary and narrative modes to choose from. Pre-dominantly there was, for example, the modernist tradition of teleological marxism – history is on our side – either in its activist modes or in its magisterial, *ex cathedra* style. It assumed that both writer and reader were as one, belonging to a common intellectual and political tradition whose time had (almost) come. Yet both variants of this dominant style – within the 'New Left' culture with which I identified – excluded any intimations of personal doubt, fallibility, or references to the actual conditions of writing. They also required that no matter how pessimistic the analysis, every essay or report should end with a call to further resolute action and debate, in much the same way that the nineteenth century symphony had to end with a return to the home key. The form at times was obviously self-defeating.

Yet this tradition had its strengths. It was a literary form that operated within, and was the expression of, a tradition of collectivist or shared political work rather than one undertaken solely in the spirit of individual, disinterested intellectual enquiry. It was often collaborative. It was also assumed to be linked unproblematically to questions of social change, and was oriented towards the future. In short, it was *engaged.*

Some people writing in Britain in this period were trying to do something different, notably, in my opinion, John Berger and Angela Carter as well as, on occasions, Ray Gosling, Jeremy Seabrook and Raphael Samuel, all associated with the magazine

New Society. These writers managed to allude to their own direct experience, while still writing within a political, historical or documentary literary tradition. There were others of course. One of them was Ian Walker, whom I knew and admired enormously, but who in some ways, I think, was destroyed by some of these very difficulties. At the time I found it impossible to write within these looser forms, the weight of my political past simply would not allow the use of the personal pronoun – widely regarded as the weak link in the critical-analytical chain. This remains a deep fault-line within social democratic politics – an inability to come to terms with notions of individual sovereignty – which is why social democracy, in my opinion, can never be sufficient to itself as a political culture, and why other radical intellectual traditions need to be cherished and sustained. Social democracy, in short, still has no aesthetic.

There was also available a wider tradition and set of assumptions about writing, notably that of post-war European humanism, again using a shared and unquestioned set of cultural references – individual existential despair, the human condition, the primacy of literary and other forms of artistic mediation, our common European home. While still ostensibly authoritative and largely impersonal, this in fact felt less like a narrative form and more like an intellectual sensibility: it was another step closer to the self. During this time I wrote poetry, which was occasionally published to my private delight and public discomfiture.

The second significant change in this enduring struggle with form happened as I began to keep a diary in my early thirties, and then to start writing long letters to friends. This was a move from the public world of articles, committee reports, essays and speeches, to the private world of individual beliefs and apprehensions, to family life, to dreams and nightmares, to friendship and other personal matters, which, slowly over time, I learned to share. The temptation was to use the confessional voice or mode, which was becoming more widely used as a result of the impact of feminism and the left's tentative exploration of psychoanalysis. Yet I hesitated and then resisted. For what I quickly came to realise was that the impulse to write personally was always linked to some kind of experience of travel. No sooner was I free of the routines of sedentary life, than I began to observe, reflect and write differently. This is not an uncommon experience, and as the critic Janet

Wolff has noted, is very much a masculine (i.e. circuitous) approach to the personal and to the unravelling of 'the self'. Vladimir Medem, a Russian writer, once said that an individual in Russia was composed of three parts: a body, a soul and a passport. These elements, I feel, make up my own conditions of writing.

About this time – in the early 1980s – I also discovered the pleasures of cycling. I was invited to take a 'proper job' at the Greater London Council for a while, and I began to cycle to work, as so many other GLC *apparatchiks* did. Cycling to work led to the occasional weekend charity ride of fifty to sixty miles. These seemed not unusually difficult and I enjoyed the company and the itineraries enormously. In 1986 I took part in a two week charity ride from John O'Groats to Land's End, some 900 miles, mostly in the rain, and by the end of that great journey I had found a new cause. I also had another reason for writing letters.

What I discovered in the habit of letter-writing was the gradual development of a narrative voice which I realise now was not that of personal confession but that of a story-teller, still keeping that connection to direct speech that letters embody. As Elzbieta Ettinger writes of Rosa Luxemburg's letters to her lover, Leo Jogiches, 'Luxemburg does not write, she speaks to him.' [2] In other fine collections of letters – those of Sartre and de Beauvoir[3], or from Václav Havel in prison to his wife, Olga[4] – the immediacy of the spoken voice and the detailed attention to everyday life and routines makes compulsive reading. The letters in this book are not quite so personal, but they are, in a sense, a way of talking to absent friends, and they may be of interest to a wider circle of people. I hope so.

Such writing is at times fraught with difficulties. Attention to the myriad and protean detail of the given world, of conversations with others, of architectural detail, of birds seen, or incidents observed, requires keeping notes – and people with notebooks are often regarded by others, with some justification, as spies. There is nothing more chilling than the line from the traditional

[2] *Comrade and Lover: Rosa Luxemburg's Letters to Leo Jogiches,* edited and translated by Elzbieta Ettinger, MIT Press, Massachusetts, 1981.

[3] *Witness to my Life: Letters from Jean-Paul Sartre to Simone de Beauvoir 1926 - 1939,* Hamish Hamilton, 1992 and *Quiet Moments in a War 1940 – 1963,* Hamish Hamilton 1994.

[4] Václav Havel, *Letters to Olga,* Faber & Faber, London 1990.

American blues song: 'There's a man going round taking names.' Many years ago I interviewed a young woman writer who had suddenly sprung to fame as the result of publishing a highly regarded first novel, yet who still lived on the council estate in Coventry where she had grown up. After her fame became known locally, whenever she walked into any of the neighbourhood shops, she told me, everybody stopped talking, and wouldn't start again until after she had gone. It was assumed that she had become some kind of recording angel at best, eavesdropper and secret agent at worst.

I would say that it is almost impossible to write in a notebook in public without considerable self-consciousness. It is, thankfully, the last taboo in a culture of free expression. Were everybody to be note-taking, photographing, and video-recording everybody else then the illusion of a pristine, existential authenticity of the moment would be lost for ever. Shame, guilt and embarrassment are proper emotions for a writer (though there are many others), and in making notes for these letters, whether on the back of beer mats, on opened-out cigarette packets, on maps, or even in notebooks, I have felt all three.

There haven't been many narrative models to express this kind of consciousness within the British literary or political tradition: the episodic, fragmented, aphoristic bricolage of the hurrying, anxious and dislocated life. The German tradition is stronger – perhaps this is because of, or is it in spite of, the fact that there was little or no nineteenth century German novel tradition, with the exception of Theodor Fontane's *Effi Briest* : at least this is what my German friends tell me. That tradition includes the satires and aphorisms of Lichtenberg, the notebooks and stories of Kafka (writing in German from Prague), Brecht's notebooks, diaries, letters, fables, poems and occasional writings (which have a liveliness and intellectual attention to detail that are continually rewarding), and the little fables and stories of Robert Walser (most famously *The Walk*), which are now held in high regard, as innovations in the modern literary consciousness. More recently there has been the work of Franz Fühmann, whose brilliant, *Twenty-Two Days or Half a Lifetime* (a travel notebook) is now translated into English. And of course there is the immensely rich, suggestive and profound work of Walter Benjamin, particularly in *One-Way Street*, which has become a modernist Talmud itself to a certain kind of contemporary intellectual and literary frame of mind. The literary sketch, the set of notebook entries, the modern fable, the fragment, are, like the cabaret song and the satirical pencil sketch, forms of what in Germany is called the *kleine kunst*, the 'little arts', that can at times be more incisive, resonant and enduring, than the larger cultural forms, particularly in times of transition and fragmentary cultural change.

These letters possess little of the expected attributes of travel writing. I have not encountered danger, nor gone away for years on end. I have not suffered privation nor been driven to the edge of madness. On the other hand, I have been mystified, I have been troubled, and I have also, on occasions, been very happy. Benjamin recounts one of Lichtenberg's aphorisms to the effect that there is always the danger that if you leave home to find the world, the world may at that very same time come to you, only to find you gone. This tension or disparity between 'here' and 'there', no longer seems the irreconcilable divide it once was. I cannot understand 'there' except in relation to 'here', any more than I can understand travel except in relation to how I live at home, and to the people I love who live there. It is what I find most suspect about much travel writing – the unanswered questions as to what kind of life and relationships the writer/traveller has left behind.

The letters which follow are arranged by theme, resisting the tyranny of chronology. They begin with the death of my father; but later on, in other letters, he is still alive. Despair and exhilaration have come and gone in equal measure at different periods of my life, though reading Havel's letters quite recently I noted with a nod of recognition that he realised that he could only write in a mood of high spirits, as I too have found. More than anything else, one needs energy to write, and energy comes with hope and the possibility of change. I am always buoyed up by a remark by Walter Benjamin – whose spirit haunts these letters – that in the end, 'all the decisive blows are struck left-handed'. These letters were written with the left hand.

Sleeper

He would travel
Disguised as an Englishman

A succession of jobs, study, then marriage
He moved to a safe house in the city

Climbed the ladder steadily
Took a different route to work each day

Cultivated friends
Established a network of contacts

Over the years he learnt
To love the native countryside

The rolling downs, the ox-bow valleys,
Dry stone walls and Norman churches

Learnt to swim in cold dark rivers
Bathe in the rusty, groaning sea

No one would guess
That behind drawn curtains, late at night

He would sift through files
Pore over government reports

Make long phone calls to other cities
Set up meetings, plan demonstrations

Type out notes from informal conversations
Study the works of murdered intellectuals

Write poems in code
Keep a diary of metaphors

Send letters abroad
Which he posted last thing at night

In the letter box by the park gates
Listening to the wind in the chestnut trees

Looking up at the stars and the moon
Half hidden by clouds

The dreams of insurrection fading
More worried about the roses in the garden

Waiting for further orders
The call to action, which never came.

1984

1 London – Brighton – Stockholm – London December 1990

I am starting this letter on the morning of my father's funeral. At noon Larraine and I will drive down to Brighton to be at the crematorium for 3.15 where the minister will conduct a short service and read out testimonies to my father from my brother, Ian, and myself, and then it will all be over. I told the minister on the phone a few days before that I was not prepared to have him, a stranger, say anything about our father – just conduct the committal service – and he agreed with that sentiment. So often I've been at funerals where the officiating minister has mouthed words of the utmost sanctimoniousness, only revealing that they never knew the person in life. I've even known them get the name wrong. I'm writing this because I can't settle to work, and somehow I want to record this enormous shift in my life as it happens. If I could write this letter in verse I would. Auden's verse letters are among the most important things that shaped my imaginative life, and which have sustained my belief in order and form, and I'm sorry I'm not up to replicating them. Prose will have to do. Auden comes to mind, too, because suddenly we are having unusually cold weather – snow in London, cancelled trains, airports shut. That was how Auden marked Yeats' funeral:

> He disappeared in the dead of winter:
> The brooks were frozen, the air-ports almost deserted,
> And snow disfigured the public statues;
> The mercury sank in the mouth of the dying day.

The minister will read what my brother has written:

> Having chosen to visit and talk to Dad while he was still with us, I've asked Ken to read a few words today in my absence. For my part I shall take a walk among the pines of the Catskills, for if there is any element I always associate with Dad, it is the scent of fresh wood. A visit to any timber yard will take me back to the days in Dad's various woodshops, and now that the time has come to summon up the abiding memory of him, I see him in his leather waistcoat and canvas apron, whistling *Buttons and Bows.* There is the sawdust from the fresh-cut wood, a folding ruler and a carpenter's pencil. If

I could, I would seal this letter with the stick of red sealing wax sitting on his office desk.

Where I am now, early in the morning, deer stroll through the garden, sunlight catches the mountain and filters through the evergreens. It's worth getting up for, which is what Dad did best. In my early teens the times we were best able to talk were the times I got up early for my paper round. He would be on his third pot of tea by then, and I would have a cup too. I know now how much he was aware of the pleasures of early morning solitude; it was on one such occasion he told me about the death of his own father.

The hours spent with Dad on different visits were filled with a wide range of emotions, from maudlin to angry to sublime; for as we all know so well, Dad was different; a manifest outsider troubled by the early death of his mother and the fragmentation of life during the war; of oblique relationships and the constant struggle to 'make a go of it'.

Without any of us really being aware of it at the time, we learned much from him. If there is one incident I recollect that shows Dad's humanity, it was the time I went with him to survey the ruins of his woodyard caused by the floods at Wickford in 1957. Gazing out at the ruined stock, water washing everywhere, some boys came up and asked if they could use some of the wood for rafts. Dad just asked them to bring it back when they were done. For many years after, life was measured in terms of before and after the flood.

Now that I live so far away, I am grateful that both of my children met their English grandfather. It means April and I, Ursula and Emma can all say, 'Goodbye Dad, we'll remember you in our different ways, and as long as we live so will you'.

Your loving son, Ian.

And what I have written:

Our father, Jack Worpole, strode a singular path through life. He was a very self-contained man, who found relationships with other people difficult at times, yet his own transparent honesty, rugged independence and battered optimism, remained among his most endearing qualities to those who knew him, certainly to his two sons. At the worst of times he was able to draw on memories and feelings of periods of great happiness, and he was always sustained by the music on the Third Programme – particularly Beethoven, Mozart,

Tchaikowsky and Elgar – which was his constant companion wherever he lived. He loved the Sussex Downs, the changing of the seasons, and had an a keen awareness of the loveliness and mystery of the natural world.

In his last years he found an inner peace which had eluded him for long periods of his life, and in his west-facing room at the rest home in Hove – with the wonderful views of the nearby gardens and of the distant sea – he came into his own. There he was looked after by the staff with great cheerfulness and affection, and in his last weeks he was also deeply moved by the love and care unstintingly given to him by the nurses and doctors of the Royal Sussex County Hospital. One of life's 'awkward squad', as he himself admitted, in life he was impossible to ignore and in death impossible to forget. My brother and I owe him a great debt.

Although I'm partly dreading it, the funeral will come as a great relief, for the past few months have been very difficult, as he had been dying slowly and miserably of cancer in hospital in Brighton, and I'd been travelling up and down to sit by the bedside and keep him company – of sorts. Luckily my brother came over from America – where he lives – for a week to see him while he was still in good spirits and mentally alert, and the both of us had some good talks on the drives to and from Brighton, reviewing our lives as we crawled along Brixton Road, straggled through Purley, and sped over the Sussex Downs in our ancient and heavily battered car.

What I couldn't have said aloud at the funeral would be that his happiest times were during the war, firstly as a wireless operator at Scapa Flow in the Orkneys for six months and later in Burma where he found a way of life and a people that he could genuinely love. He never saw actual combat. In the Orkneys he had his own small rowing boat and he rowed from ship to ship repairing wirelesses, returning at night to a hut of his own and the Third Programme. It was a posting that nobody wanted and which after six months they had to tear him away from. He was obviously happiest away from women – he told me he was shy about 'girls' as a young man – and unfortunately this developed into a bitter misogyny after our parents' marriage failed (of course it was also a contributory factor), and it was only as a patient in the two rest homes he finally settled in, and in his last days in hospital, that he was able to enjoy the company of women near him, affectionate, bantering, but wholly without sexual threat. In fact he was captivated by several of the young women who nursed him in his last year, and they in turn I know found him loveable and strangely innocent. For the second half of his life he lived in a succession of lodging houses and rooms, fiercely independent, and when not working as a carpenter he either drank alone in Kemptown pubs or lay on his bed listening to Radio 3. One standing joke I always had with him was to ask him if he'd recently listened to *Music in Our Time*, a weekly programme on Thursday evenings devoted to contemporary music. 'They can't be serious can they, Ken? It's just noises, bangs, sounds more like interference in the airwaves than music. Load of bloody nonsense, I ask you.' If I'd have hated him I would have played *Konzertstücke für Synthesiser, Ring Modulator and Tape Loop Opus 4* at his funeral; instead it's Mozart and Vaughan Williams. Will he ever know?

Music is a great lightener and healer. I can never fail to be cheered by putting on a tape or record of African dance music and sashaying around the attic room where I (mostly) work – even at the worst of times. Larraine and I recently enjoyed an inspiring evening at The Royal Festival Hall where the Siobhan Davies Dance Company performed to two modern string quartet pieces – Kevin Volans' *White Man Sleeps* and Steve Reich's *Different Trains* – both played by the Smith Quartet. It was, I think, one of my happiest concert-going evenings ever, particularly so because we were both a bit down and depressed. Bruce Chatwin listened incessantly to Volans' *White Man Sleeps* as he was dying of AIDS, and there's an essay about Volans in Chatwin's posthumous collected journalism, *What Am I Doing Here?*

When we got back from the funeral and after taking Ben and Anna out for a meal (in lieu of a wake), we sat and chatted, and listened to the Modern Jazz Quartet's film score *No Sun in Venice.* The track *The Golden Striker* contains a piano solo by John Lewis of austere and haunting beauty, quite without compare. The MJQ were over-rated, then under-rated, but at their best they contributed something permanent to the jazz canon, and some of Lewis' compositions and elegant piano playing are as subtle and finely modulated and expressive as anything by Debussy. The film for which it was an original score is a post-war black and white Italian story set against the fading stucco and ruined campaniles of Venice. They don't make post-war films like that anymore.

The funeral was made bearable by the surroundings: a walled garden and redbrick Lutyens type building set in a hollow in the Downs near Brighton. The brass gleamed, the oak woodwork shone with polish; there were flowers and stained glass everywhere. It was the last funeral of the day and everybody seemed to have gone home. Larraine and I arrived to find what seemed to be an open but deserted country house. Then the hearse arrived, with the benign canon whom I'd tipped off about not saying anything of his own; just follow the script, in other words. He was very nice and though it was a bit absurd, Larraine and I making up the complete congregation, failing also to join in any of the hymns and prayers because we were locked into our own thoughts, he really was sincere about the whole thing. At one point shortly before he commended our father to God, like a school report, he ventured to suggest that Jack Worpole might already be with God, even though the coffin so materially and solidly lay there before us. Some transformation; some quick change scene.

I was slightly detached from the whole thing because all emotion had already been expended. This leaden-skied, cold December afternoon was a relief; a clear stream. It was so dark with impending snow that even at noon the cars were lumbering up and down the A23 with their headlights on, as though they were all coming to the funeral. The nightmare had been seeing my father's body the day after he died, in the hospital Chapel of Rest, and barely being able to recognise the ravaged, jaundiced and shrivelled body flat out on a covered table like an unburied cathedral knight. After that absolute realisation that he was dead, the days after were like swimming back to the surface. I'm very glad I saw him like that; it was a tumultuous shock but it was also the turning point in the whole miserable but unavoidable affair.

There were no last words, no final perorations on life's mixed blessings. He refused to talk about dying, though he obviously knew he was. Where one desperately wanted him to slowly and hesitantly issue forth greetings and final last wishes to grandchildren, to make summing up speeches and final soliloquies, all he ever managed were some worried words about not forgetting to collect a pair of slippers he'd left at the home because 'there's still a lot of wear in them yet.' He was also worried in case the nurses took his new pyjamas away before he got the chance to wear them. In his last weeks heavily sedated with morphine, he occasionally broke the surface of consciousness with strange observations, one time remarking that 'the colours in their faces make them look better'; another time saying that he had dreamed of London buses, or of a gold prospector in Australia, and even one Saturday afternoon, when he could not possibly have known what day of the week it was, asking how West Ham did today? The nurses and doctors were beyond conventional praise. Their kindness, care and disinterested love for their elderly patients belongs to another world than the one the rest of us inhabit every day of the year. Closed worlds of love and solicitude. Why are the rest of us so permanently locked out?

* * *

It's some days later. The day before Christmas Eve in fact. There were a couple of wretched domestic jobs I had to do before Christmas – put washers on leaking taps, re-cement a grille that had fallen out of the front of the house just under the front doorstep – so being Sunday I got on my bike and cycled down to our neighbourhood builders' merchants in our road which is strictly kosher and therefore open on Sundays. All the men serving in the shop and in the yard – lugging bags of cement, cutting up timber, sorting through the washers and screws – wear either yarmulkes or black Homburgs on their heads and full prayer shawls under their aprons. They are an incredibly cheerful lot, and tell terrible jokes to customers which they laugh at loudly among themselves. I always enjoy going there. It's interesting, you don't get any of the swearing there that you usually get in builders' merchants, even though most of their customers are Irish and East London cowboys. Next door, in the window of the Tandoori restaurant, is a notice which says, 'Sorry to our customers, we are closed for some reason.'

* * *

My father's illness made planning difficult for a while. I convinced myself it was right to go ahead with a trip to Stockholm in November, planned for some time, as the doctor thought he'd get through that particular week. It was an extraordinary trip, packed with incident, though I telephoned the hospital every day while I was out there. I had been doing some work on urban design and public transport systems, and had managed to arrange a visit to see a number of public art programmes in Stockholm, particularly that based on the underground system, and to talk with the designers and commissioning agencies. The Stockholm underground is famous for the extensive decoration of its subways and stations, described as, at 92 kilometres, 'the longest art gallery in the world'.

I'd arranged to stay with a woman friend whom Larraine and I had met in London in the early 1970s when she ran a British-Swedish adult education joint study programme, and we'd got on very well. Even when we'd known her in London she was very hard working and a touch eccentric in the best of senses. Five days staying in her house convinced me she was a new kind of post-political saint. I arrived at her house at night by train and then taxi; she'd gone out to a meeting. As the taxi headlights swept through a very leafy almost rural suburb, lighting up the big timber houses with their summer houses, gardens going down to the lakes that were everywhere, bumping up and down the unmade roads, the driver pulled up at one that looked like a building site, with old lorries outside and the garden completely overgrown. Somehow I knew this was hers. She was obviously the sort of person (exactly like my father in fact) who within weeks of moving anywhere had the neighbours signing petitions against them, seeking their eviction, transfer or removal. In my father's case it was because wherever we lived he always turned every square foot of garden space or frontage into a timber yard. In the case of Astrid, it transpired, it was because she had a habit of fostering, adopting or simply befriending young homeless people, immigrants and orphans, who invariably earned their living as lorry-drivers, car mechanics or failed landscape contractors. Her select suburban residential house had become a permanent job creation scheme. In the five days I was there – she woke me at 5.30 every morning with an even more strenuous programme of meetings than was humanly possible – I was always bumping into strange young men and women in the bathroom, sauna, kitchen, garden, front room, everywhere. These were her 'children'. She'd saved them from drugs, suicide attempts, forced marriages, alcoholism, street gangs, and most surprisingly of all, everyone had made good. They adored her. She was completely non-judgmental. 'Ken. I say to my children, you can't hurt me any more than you can hurt yourself. If you steal from me I give you more. If you burn my house down (one of them almost did), I will build you another. Ken, we must love everybody, that is what socialism is about. But ach, here in Sweden, socialism is about men in suits. The real socialism is people, Ken, people living their lives to do good to each other. You understand me?'

She had encouraged two of her 'children' to train as taxi-drivers by training alongside them in her spare time. She had set another up as a landscaping contractor by letting him experiment on her garden and use it as a yard. Another one, who had the room next to mine, was always trying money-making schemes. One day he brought home two minks and planned to breed them in his room. By the first evening the smell permeated the whole house, but Astrid let him carry on until the scheme collapsed. They repaired motor bikes in their bedrooms, and fired hunting guns from the balcony. And Astrid just took it all in her stride. She was, I discovered, deeply religious. She went to whatever church was closest at the time – Protestant, Catholic, Jewish – and had a formidable reputation in the Labour Party and Trade Union establishment for having her say.

A couple of years ago, she told me one evening, she had taken a new boyfriend, an amiable electrician with a bit of a drink problem, but that would have been typical of her. Another working-class soul to be saved. They had been meeting for several months before at last they decided to go to bed with each other. (She told me every detail of this story). She had cooked supper for them both at the house, drunk several bottles of wine, and called out goodnight to whoever was in the house and went to her room. As soon as they had got into bed one of the 'children', a 24 year old lorry-driver, got into bed between them. '"But Goran", I said, "Åke and I want to go to sleep." "No", he said, "We don't think it is a good idea." And he just lay there refusing to move. You see, Ken, of course they were jealous, and I have to understand this strong feelings they have. Ach, it how easily we are hurting each other, if we don't explain everything and talk about it.' Is this not the patience of a saint? The long view?

My programme was a series of meetings with arts administrators who put art into public places – hospitals, factories, schools, parks and gardens and public transport. That programme had been arranged by the Swedish Institute, but Astrid looked at the programme and wondered why I was only working seven hours a day. She doubled it with a few phone calls, getting me to a dinner party with the Director of the Swedish Arts Council and the Polish Cultural Ministry chief who was visiting, a theatre party with the leaders of the Swedish TUC to see a classic play of the labour movement lasting three hours in Swedish, to talk to the student leaders of 1968 who were now running youth and homeless projects in the suburbs, and a few other things. She simply picked up the phone and it happened. The pace of her life – and the productiveness of it – gave the lie to Oscar Wilde's sympathetic assertion that the problem with socialism is that there aren't enough evenings in the week. For some people, there are.

Astrid, not surprisingly, was a 'Mother of the Night'. The 'Mothers' and 'Fathers of the Night' are parents who volunteer to walk the streets of Stockholm at weekends befriending the many hundreds of runaway, homeless or out of control teenagers who hang around MacDonalds or the Central Station drinking, mugging and fighting. Sometimes they take them somewhere for coffee; sometimes they take them home. This laudable 'citizen's initiative' belies the widespread assumption that in Sweden people leave the state to solve everything.

One of the places they might end up in is the *Fryshuset*, a giant meat-packing factory and refrigerated warehouse two bus stops from the city centre, now converted into what must be the largest youth project in Europe. Astrid took me there. The *Fryshuset* contains 52 rooms converted to rehearsal studios, where 156 different rock and jazz bands rehearse each week, as well as a sports hall, three performance venues, a coffee bar, a skate-boarding hall, a music school, a drama school and 'comprehensive free school' that copes with the most difficult of the young people who use the centre – when I visited the latter there were thirteen pupils and six staff. The *Fryshuset* was the brainchild of Anders Carlberg, one of the student leaders of Sweden's own tumultuous 1968, and at least half of the people I talk to during my visit refer to 'the lessons we learned from 1968', a far cry from Britain where the left today seems even more embarrassed by memories of student impossibilism and utopian politics than of the leaden Wilson years.

Only by scaling up Sweden's population to that of Britain can one fully appreciate the measure of some of social democracy's most significant cultural achievements. The *Litteraturframjandet* (Literature for All) project is a subsidised publishing house specialising in providing 'quality' books to schools, factories, adult study circles and nurseries. Many of these books are Swedish literary classics, novels of working-class life, as well as translations of books by James Joyce, Isaac B. Singer, Doris Lessing, Barbara Pym, Heinrich Böll among others. Twenty titles a year are published, along with twenty children's books, in editions of 25,000 each. To get some idea of what this means one would have to imagine our Arts Council funding an independent publishing house to produce a series of paperback novels by writers such as Dickens, Conrad, Virginia Woolf and Orwell, together with translations of books by Cora Sandel, Christa Wolf and August Strindberg, in print runs of 175,000 copies, each title to be distributed by the TUC. There's a challenge.

State cultural policy has been developed to meet the distinctive historical, geographical and demographic characteristics of Swedish life. In a large country with a small population, a co-ordinated network of public libraries, subsidised book clubs, writers' bursaries and grant-aided publishing houses has been established to do the job that in the UK commercial bookselling and publishing claims to do. Over 60 per cent of Swedish people use the public library system; more books are sold by mail than through shops. Support for literature is one of the most developed areas of subsidised activity, though there is also an 'Art for All' scheme and a 'Theatre for All' initiative which commission artists, playwrights and theatres to produce works for community, trade union and workplace audiences. 'Theatre for All' has a national network of over 10,000 workplace organisers selling tickets and organising plays.

All these organisations are knitted into what clearly remains a powerful and traditional 'labour movement'. When I asked a friend of Astrid's who works at the Swedish TUC about this he gave me a wry smile and said that 'The reason we're still here is that we bureaucratised the movement – party, unions, workers' education, culture – they're all funded by the state. We can outlast any recession.' Yet this doesn't equate with one-party hegemony. Freedom of expression is the first principle of cultural policy, and involves, for example, an annual government subsidy of over £60 million to sustain a politically bi-partisan regional press. Without this social democratic policy, the conservative daily *Svenska Dagbladet* would have gone to the wall, a victim of market forces.

And although the language of Swedish social democracy sometimes 'tastes too much of concrete', as my old friend, Per, who works at the *Kulturhuset* put it to me, the need for a powerful cultural infrastructure of a subsidised press, cinema, theatre, music, adult education system, libraries and folk-husets is accepted by all political parties. Without subsidy and regulation, I was told, Swedish language and culture could disappear within two generations.

Participation in adult education is even more pronounced with some 2.6 million adults out of a total population of 8.4 million involved, confirming Olaf Palme's famous saying that 'Swedish democracy is built on life in study circles.' Yet the old Social Democratic hegemony is in trouble. The Social Democrats have never fully recovered from Palme's murder in 1986, a shock to the system which was exacerbated by the incompetent police investigation which followed. Perhaps only one detective could have solved Palme's murder, Inspector Martin Beck of the Stockholm Police, yet sadly he was just the fictional creation of writers Maj Sjöwall and Per Wahloo, whose Stockholm detective novels remain among the best evocations of this intriguing city. Meanwhile the fashion among Swedish young men still favours the tightly belted white trenchcoat, giving the impression of a city full of gumshoes, combing the streets for clues to a missing ideology.

My visit finished with a trip I've always wanted to make again – to the Stockholm archipelago, a loose jigsaw puzzle of 17,000 islands which go from Stockholm into the Baltic Sea, and on which many hundreds of thousands of families have their summer houses. This is Pippi Longstocking country, and also of Strindberg's nineteenth century crazed peasants and fishermen; I'd sailed through them before, in 1964. This time Astrid was taking me out to their island where Ake was building a summer cottage for the two of them, and it was another 5.30 am start. We were going just for the day. The ferry left Stockholm at 7.30 am and it was a three-and-a-half hour trip, some 60 miles out into the Baltic, but never more than two hundred yards away from at least six islands. Each island is perfectly formed, some only 50 yards across with just the one cottage, and they are simply outcrops of pink granite, with a sparse and rough vegetation of pine and fir trees, seagrass, juniper bushes and brambles. And there are a myriad of landing jetties with boats of all sizes tied up. It was a rough, windy overcast day, the water grey and choppy; in the summer this must be dreamlike, cutting through the blue-green waters, with the red ochre cottages, the pink islands, and the white sailing boats everywhere on the water.

The ferry was full. I suppose there were about a hundred people in all. And the mood changed very quickly as we left Stockholm, for I began to understand why the summer islands (even in winter) are so important to the Swedish psyche. For firstly, although there are strict rules about alcohol on the mainland – basically it is almost impossible to get outside of very expensive hotels – on the ferries you can drink as much as you want. Some people, I'm told, spend their weekends in the bar on a return ticket to Helsinki. So even though a can of beer cost £3.50, they were queuing up as soon as the mooring ropes were untied and cast off. I had a couple of cans of beer and a cheese roll for breakfast, and felt rather enlivened and adventurous for it. Astrid, who never drank during the week, drank half a bottle of Valpolicella by 8 am and then slept for the rest of the journey. The sturdy, sober burghers of Stockholm turn into bohemian rebels once they are on board a ferry and off to the islands.

Ours was one of the last ports of call, a creaking wooden jetty with Åke waving cheerily on it. A dream landscape: water and islands, islands and water. It was a fifteen minute walk through the woods to the half-built cottage, passing a number of old wooden seamen's cottages on the way. There were 200 houses on the islands but in only eight of them were there original island families still living: people whose parents and grandparents had spent all their lives living a traditional peasant and sea-fishing economy only 60 miles from the capital of advanced social democracy and twenty-first century lifestyles. We passed the cottage of Captain Rose. Rose was his first name. 'Yes. It's the same in Swedish; why his mother called him Rose nobody knows, but it is rather lovely idea don't you think?' Yes, I do. Captain Rose was away on a long trip. Someone else was looking after his ten cats. When at home he sits in a rocking chair drinking home-distilled *akavit* with a cat sitting on each shoulder 'to keep his rheumatism away'. That's another true story.

This island idyll reminded me of that portrayed in Malcolm Lowry's collection *Hear Us O Lord From Heaven Thy Dwelling Place.* In his case, the island was in the Vancouver estuary where Lowry and his wife lived during the war on a wooden hut on stilts, in an exiled community of fishermen, seamen and recluses, and represented for Lowry the paradisal aspects of his life compared to the hell of his alcoholic nightmare in Mexico, both of which are described in *Under the Volcano.* I first came across Lowry, who for a while was my first and last literary hero, mentor and psychological fixation, when I bought a second-hand copy of *New World Writing* in Collets on my way to the Tilbury Docks to take the boat to Gothenberg, when I went 'on the road' in 1964. In it I found Lowry's serene story, 'The Forest Footpath to the Spring', that had led me to read everything he wrote, and here, 26 years later the story had come full circle.

There was just enough time to have lunch, inspect Åke's small boat and walk in the woods before catching the 3pm return ferry. If there had been one. Oh yes, we got there and waited for some while on the windy jetty with the sky darkening rapidly before Åke looked at the hand-painted timetable on the waiting room hut only to discover that there wasn't a return ferry on Saturday. Sunday, yes, Saturday, no. My plane left for London early the following morning. And here I stood, on an island in the Baltic, only the wind and the water roaring all around me, all exit routes closed. But Astrid and Åke didn't worry at all. They would ask Åke's friend, another fisherman, to take us two islands' distance, where we could catch a bus, believe it or not. If he was sober. (Åke's boat was unseaworthy.) Lars was still sober, though he had a garden shed that had more retorts, tubes, condensers and barrels for making illegal *akavit* than the ICI works at Billingham. And an hour later I was standing in a tiny open boat, in the complete darkness, being hurtled across the Baltic waves, tossed up and down like a fairground ride, to another island connected to the mainland by two short distance ferries that operated hourly throughout the year. I'd asked about life-jackets. Not worth it, Åke had replied nonchalantly, you'd only last three minutes in the water, life-jacket or not. Another debt from my past repaid. I had always vowed to visit the archipelago again.

It had been nearly eight years since I had last seen Astrid. Like all of us her features had changed, relaxing into familial shapes and gestures. It was Astrid who, when she talked about her own family, asked if I had noticed her Mongolian features. For the first time I had. Her parents were Samis – genuine Lapps – originally from Asia. She was inordinately proud of her genuine peasant origins. Sophisticate of the labour movement higher echelons though she was, a good mixer (mostly) in higher Swedish society, she returned three or four times a year to her parents in Swedish Lapland, bringing home with her fresh carcasses of deer which she would butcher at home and pack into her freezer. She had to have reindeer meat, she said. When young she had once swallowed a bone and was in danger of dying; her father had severed her windpipe with his knife and saved her. One of her fingers had been cut off in an accident; her father had sewed it back on. She showed me the scar. In the region of her childhood it was completely dark for 60 days of the winter solstice. They lived 50 miles from the nearest town.

Swedish society is only two generations away from peasant society; this I was told time and time again. The writer Stig Dagerman wrote in *A Child's Memoirs* that what he remembered most about the Stockholmers who visited his grandparents' cottage where he lived as a young boy was that they used the word 'also': clear evidence of another, more sophisticated, world. Property rights have been deeply affected by this attachment to the land and the countryside. I'd asked Astrid how come that all the islands hadn't been bought as private property. Many of the smaller ones had, she said. But in Sweden, owning property does not give you any rights to deny access to other people. It doesn't matter that an island is privately owned; everybody else has the right to land there, camp (for one night only) or regularly visit it, have picnics and simply hang out. Swedish law allows anybody to camp for one night only anywhere in Sweden – in your neighbour's garden, on Swedish army property (I continue to doubt this); simply anywhere, I'm told.

It was a memorable trip. Stockholm is a beautiful city, with fabulous eighteenth century fortresses, castles and apartment houses solidly built on a network of granite islands, between which the lighted ferries appear to glide all evening. Some of them are giant boats which daily cross the Baltic between Stockholm and Helsinki carrying workers in both directions, and which at night drift into the heart of the city like floating pieces of Manhattan. Soon, everybody assumes, they will be carrying Russians. Much of the newer development is a dismal failure, and again leaves unresolved the problem of whether there is yet such a thing as an established social democratic architectural style or tradition. Why is the older stuff so good?

An up and down year in many ways, like the boat ride between the islands. I was feeling whole again after my father's funeral when the very next morning I opened the papers to read the obituary of the journalist and writer, Ian Walker, whom I had known and liked greatly in the 1970s. He was only 38. He'd fallen from a tenement balcony in a fatal mood of drink and paranoia, apparently, just as his mother and some friends were arriving to take him to hospital. Someone who rang me that night said, 'Ian was the last person you would have thought might be tempted to kill himself,' but if you read his account of a two year sojourn in Berlin, *Zoo Station*, the clouds of monumental despair were already blotting out the sky. It is one of the best contemporary pieces of autobiographical writing I know, but it is hopelessly ill-starred, romantic and doomed. I last saw him at the packed lecture given by Rudolf Bahro who was over from the GDR to speak in the wake of the success of his book, *The Alternative.* I guess it was 1980. He was, as always, dressed as 'the English boy' as his German friends called him, in a Fred Perry tennis shirt, Staprest trousers and Dr Martens, someone who had never stopped being a 'mod'. I followed him through his writings for years after, and I think he was among the best writers that the left produced in the 1970s and 1980s.

Parents, friends, heroes: in time we lose them all, or they lose us. That's why writing has been so important for me. Every time I start one of these letters I drag myself to the typewriter or word processor in front of me, daunted by the effort ahead, surrounded by scraps of papers, notes, lines and snatches of conversation written on beermats and exhibition catalogues. Yet when I have finished, days, even weeks later, I feel that I have erected some kind of permanent memorial to all these good, if sometime difficult, people; to all those eventful, sometime drunken evenings, to all those bleak thoughts or moments of sheer happiness. I want to remember everything.

2 London – Brighton – Tuscany June 1991

Early yesterday morning we were woken by the very loud warbling of a song-thrush in the top branches of a flowering cherry tree in the overgrown and abandoned garden next door. It was a continuous medley of calls, signature tunes, parodies, middle-eights, codas, grace notes, street cries and God knows what else. It wasn't difficult to spot it high up in the thinning branches, but I was surprised to see it there two hours later, exactly in the same spot, still trilling away. Two days later it is still there: its single-mindedness, energy and querulous passion remain undimmed. Because it's been out there singing for two days, we are conscious of it all the time, and no doubt will remember this spring because of the song-thrush who came to stay.

I can't write without mentioning birds – because of this attic room, because of the garden it looks out on (and the small overgrown copse beyond it) and the reservoirs that lay just beyond. One cannot but be conscious of that teeming world of birdlife that lies just on the other side of the open window, in the heart of urban, cosmopolitan London. Ducks, geese, herons, swifts, swallows, thrushes, blackbirds, magpies, jays, crows, pigeons, gulls, sparrows, starlings, tits, are all regularly seen overhead or in the nearby trees and gardens; bullfinches, goldfinches, long-tailed tits are more occasional visitors. Just the other day, on my way to the underground station at Manor House very early in the morning, I passed the reservoir: on the other side of the railings, less than 15 feet away, was a full grown heron standing at the water's edge. And this in the heart of London – a heron with an inner London postcode and two nearby underground stations to choose from. A recent wildlife survey of the Stoke Newington reservoir identified great crested grebes, little grebes, Slavonian grebes, tufted ducks, pochards, ruddy ducks, moorhens, coots, shovellers, black-headed gulls, common gulls and herring gulls as well as the swans, herons, Canada geese and mallards that fly daily over our garden to our continual delight. Some ecologists are now claiming that there is increasing bio-diversity in cities, rather than in rural areas, as a result of the use of pesticides in the countryside. We always mark the beginning of summer by the arrival of the swifts in the second week of May. At night we can often hear owls.

I am still slowly coming to terms with my father's death, consciously and unconsciously. I didn't think the impact would be so great. I now realise that he towered above my early life like a terrifying but occasionally benign giant, full of sound and fury, but with a desperate integrity of his own making. A few weeks ago when my brother came over with his family from America for a visit, he and I went down to Brighton to collect the old man's ashes and scatter them on the Sussex Downs. It was a surprisingly uplifting experience.

We drove to Brighton in a shared mood of trepidation and anxiety. But we talked a lot, and, as always, agreed that we had completely different memories of the same childhood experiences: where he saw attempted affection, I remembered anger; where he recollected periods of tranquillity, I evoked nightmares; where he forgave, I judged and found wanting. Calling in at the Co-op Funeral Parlour on the outskirts of Brighton, I was initially shocked to discover how many ashes it seemed there were. I had imagined being handed a small, symbolic urn the size of a cup or small jar. Instead we were asked to sign for a fairly large cardboard box containing a brown plastic urn the size of a boiled sweet jar, which rather unnerved me. My brother coped with it rather better.

Anyway we drove out to near Alfriston, parked at a well known beauty spot known locally as 'The Top of the World' where a few elderly couples were sitting in their cars eating sandwiches, and walked along a hilltop path carrying our box until we found a fine view of the downs, the Cuckmere river and its ox-bow meanderings, and a distant prospect of the sea. We took it in turns throwing the ashes up into the air and watching them blow on the wind and sift down into the chalky grass, and then sat down and said nothing for a few minutes. We took a last look at the valley and the downs and it was finally all over. All those years of anxiety, rage, love, benevolence, disturbance, madness – that formidable figure who bullied us into life and into nonconformity, all those strange flats and houses, kitchens, garages, sheds, timberyards, lorry cabins, pub interiors, all those memories – now entirely vanished from the material world. Puff, a life blown away on the wind like dust or a sudden shower that's dried before you even noticed it.

The triumph of the immaterial; a long physical journey lasting 76 years suddenly become an idea and a shared memory. Why shouldn't we all aspire to the condition of air? We had a couple of pints and lunch at a pub nearby and then we were back on the road to London, our arms resting on the car windows, the breeze and sun blowing through the car. Not a bad ending.

Yet I remain possessed. When I look in the mirror in the morning to shave I often see his face; sometimes when I hear myself speaking it's his intonations and cadences I hear. Because he is no longer there, embodied in the real world, I realise physically he is now embodied in me. It will pass I'm sure. Yet that's how it is: when people ring up and Ben answers they assume it is me – he sounds exactly the same. We are all carrying someone else in some form or another, like St Christopher with the weary traveller on his back. But mostly we are carrying our ghostly familiars on the inside. As I say, possessed.

My mother, always good-natured and tolerant in recent years, now occasionally complains. I think she too realises that her time is nearly up; her legs and circulation are giving way fast and now the walk to the shops is becoming an ordeal. It is not surprising that people do become bitter in old age; what else is there to do but envy the young and those with plenty of time left; how tenaciously even the most self-assured or cynical cling to world of the living, terrified to let go. As Sartre once remarked, in the end, conscious of the growing disparity between the alertness of the mind and the failure of the body, we all subscribe to traditional Christian dualism.

Unlike my mother, with strangers I'm happy to stay on the surface of things. But I know that over the years she has told the most intimate details of her life story to people at bus stops, at the hairdresser's, or in doctors' waiting-rooms: things about her life that we her sons will never know. If I had to write her biography I would have the impossible task of tracing all the women who have stood at bus stops in Romford, Chelmsford, Stratford and Bow in the last 40 years. In turn other people have spilled out their life stories to her in the most graphic detail, mostly while waiting for the 106 or the Number 5, Aldgate to Barking. When she lived in Romford and used to visit us in Stoke Newington, her opening words were all about the waiting times for the buses and the terrible life stories of the people she'd met. 'I really felt sorry for this woman, waiting for the bus at Gardiner's Corner. Her first husband died when he was only 31, then she met another chap who turned out to be an alcoholic, then she married a second time and now he's in hospital waiting to have both his legs amputated after an accident at work. And both her children have gone to live in Australia. Some people have rotten luck.' But what did you tell her, I always mean to ask? In which Poplar front room is the Worpole family history being recounted down to the last grisly detail before the kettle goes on? Is there anybody happy out there?

* * *

Though I keep a notebook I am not a writer. But describing what I do for a living is difficult, and this is always one of the main problems when I go on a long cycling trip with a group of strangers, which I've been doing regularly for the past few years, mostly abroad. The first question people ask is: and what do you do in the way of work? Well a bit of journalism, a bit of local government work, a bit of research for the Labour Party. Freelance writing, that sort of thing. But writing about what? Well, the arts, cities, things like that. What, you're a critic? No I write about arts policy? Arts policy – what's that? And so on and so forth. It all sounds so pretentious. Other people on my most recent trip cycling in Tuscany and Umbria had real jobs: railway-fitters, reflexologists, civil engineers, legal secretaries, studio photographers, psychotherapists, hairdressers, teachers. I was the only one who couldn't actually describe what I did – a good definition of a writer perhaps.

Occupation is of course the most convenient shorthand for social identity. At the start of these cycling trips, when dozens of people are milling about at Victoria Station, or some other gathering point, with their bikes and panniers, newspapers and canned drinks, mostly strangers to each other, everybody is covertly sizing each other up. Towards the end of a trip, one of a small group of women I subsequently came to spend a lot of time cycling with, explained how she had decided in which carriage to sit as we took the boat-train for the beginning of our journey to Pisa: 'I walked along the train until I came to a carriage with at least two women in with short hair and dangly earrings – that was the carriage for me.' And it worked. For her.

Often the people you sit with or get talking to in the first few hours are the people convention expects you to befriend for the duration of the trip. On the John O'Groats to Land's End ride I shared the first night in a couchette on the train going from Euston to Inverness with the most tediously obsessive man I have ever met in my life, and he clung to me for the rest of the holiday. A desperately lonely man he could only talk about his job as a heating engineer: which department he worked in, how the department was mis-managed, his missed promotion opportunities, the disrespect and apathy of the younger workers, his inappropriate car allowance, and other minutiae of his daily life, elaborated in such detail that I was reduced to a gibbering wreck. In the end I ran whenever I saw him coming towards me.

I now know in general that on these cycling tours I prefer the company of women to men, and of younger people to those chronologically my own age. Many of the women who come on these rides share a common interest in contemporary fiction, in art history, an interest in the flora and fauna, or in the domestic and working lives of the people whose countries we are cycling through; they also have no interest in cycling competitively or ridiculously fast. And I am a quite slow cyclist. I also know that in middle age I have become a deeply domestic person: a tidier of things, a cleaner, a sorter, a kitchen-lover and a jam-jar economist. And I like writing letters. It is nearly always the women on these rides who write in notebooks and send postcards. So do I. In the evenings, therefore, when walking into the camp bar after putting up the tent, setting the alarm, having a shower and locking up my bike, I would prefer to sit at a table with a mixed group where the table is loaded down with guide-books, maps, postcards, letters, as well as beer. That's how it was.

The itinerary was a circular tour of Tuscany and Umbria, camping in many of the most famous and beautiful hill-towns and cities in the Apennines, starting at Pisa and ending in Florence. In between we went through Siena, San Gimignano, Orvieto, Lago di Bolsena, Assisi, Gubbio, Citti del Castella, among others. It was a long cycle ride through an astonishing but troubled landscape, a ride that crossed many plains and valleys during the day but invariably descended and ascended some very severe hills and mountains in the mornings and evenings. The towns were strung out on the hills like beacons.

Even for Tuscany it turned out to be an unusually hot June and there were problems right from the start with the scorching temperatures after midday. Only a couple of weeks before, we were told, it had been overcast and cold. The first two afternoons turned into nightmares for most of us, struggling to cycle in temperatures in the upper 80s and early 90s, without shade, out there on the plains and on the exposed hill climbs. So adjustments were made to the timetable. We – mostly – got up about 6.15, took our tents down, had breakfast, packed and were on the road by 7.30 am, cycling the 50 miles a day before lunch-time. In the afternoons people either slept out in the fields on the route, dozed in thirteenth century churches or shaded town squares, or got to the camp and swam in the pool or lake where there was one, or hung out at the bar drinking ice-cold Peroni beers. On average I drank two and a half litres of water each morning while cycling, and only ate a couple of cheese rolls, some dried fruit and nuts, and stopped for a couple of expresso coffees. For once in the last decade I lost weight. In the end I realised I thrived in the heat, as long as there was plenty of water to drink and the bike went OK. Happy, in fact, as a pig in shit.

A number of people were there because of their interest in art history. Although that wasn't uppermost in my mind when I decided to go, by the end of the ride I really did feel that at last I understood what all the intellectual excitement was about concerning the Italian Renaissance or *Quattrocento.* I had with me, always, the *Rough Guide to Italy*, which after two weeks was almost in tatters through use. Not only did it describe each town and city in detail, opening times of galleries, best cheap cafes, and so on, but there were also long sections on Italian political and cultural history, biographies of the great artists, and hundreds of pages of other topographical, historical and contextual information. It makes a difference whether one travels through a landscape with informed eyes, or whether one travels culturally blind. As always some people (mostly men) cycled across the landscape with their eyes on the road, and only looked up when they were inside a camp bar. It could have been Uxbridge rather than Umbria for all it mattered. Yet these were in a tiny minority, more than ever, and it was interesting that for the first time on any of these trips, it was realised – and became a topic for discussion – that women cyclists out-numbered men. This really is a sea-change in cycling culture.

The 500 mile tour gave me an understanding of those great advances in painting techniques and the rise of humanism in art, that many years of reading never quite made clear. But I realise that I am someone who desperately needs to see things before I understand them. Year by year the visual, sensual, quotidian world grows in importance for me, compared with the world of abstract ideas. I can read any numbers of papers on the demographic, social and political make-up of Bolton, Middlesbrough, or Swansea, listen to talks about it, and be briefed on the town until I'm ready to drop – but I always learn more from a half-an-hour walking through the town centre, observing the people and the theatre of everyday life, and having egg and chips in the bus station cafe. I suppose I'm a doubting Thomas, an intellectual sceptic. I have to see in order to believe.

On this trip I saw enough religious frescoes and paintings to last a lifetime. By the end I had seen probably more than a hundred crucifixions, a hundred madonnas and child, nearly fifty martyrdoms of Saint Sebastian, and countless other allegorical and genre paintings of scenes from the Bible complete with God and thousands of cherubs leaning out of the sky in a golden blaze of clouds and sunbeams. But what I was able to 'see' with my own eyes and understand at last, were the sudden and decisive developments made by Giotto and other painters of the thirteenth and fourteenth centuries in moving from flat, iconic paintings of idealised but featureless Christs, Marys, Peters and Johns, to more shadowed, rounded, more introspective and haunted – at last genuinely human – representations of these religious faces, full of doubt, worry, apprehension and occasionally hope.

The frescoes were stunning. Every inch of every wall in some of the churches and cathedrals was filled with colour, light, and beautifully painted episodes from the Bible. Some could give you nightmares to last a lifetime, exactly the intention I assume, thus keeping people in the prison of their own fear and trembling, and bent to the power of the priests and the landed gentry. In Pisa, in the *Camposanto*, a thirteenth century cloistered cemetery on the north side of the *Campo dei Miracoli* (the Field of Miracles), there is a fresco of the *Triumph of Death* painted in the aftermath of the Black Death. It originally ran the length of nearly a quarter of a mile, and is filled with fires, snakes, severed members, pitchforks, babies torn limb from limb, women eaten by monsters and crushed by rocks, men being flayed and cut into pieces, that could not be looked at continuously, without the urgent desire to avert one's gaze from the suffering and torment displayed. In these matters I had already learnt my lesson. Many years ago I went to an exhibition of paintings by Hieronymous Bosch in Munich, in the Alte Pinakotek, and had nightmares afterwards that I'll never forget. Occasionally there was humour or a bit of light relief: Noah blind drunk and showing everything as he lay naked beneath a table; St Francis preaching to the birds, and some rather knowing and pretty cherubs at the edges of some of the paintings who might be doing a double take, or even winking at the artist or spectator.

There were several that I shall always remember. The first was a Nativity scene by Botticelli in the Uffizi Gallery in Florence which showed the conventional – if rather well painted – crowd gathered round the manger looking suitably awed and devotional, yet just in one corner is a well-wisher whose attention has wandered and he is staring straight into the eye of the painter or on-looker. The effect is deeply unsettling. A Breughel crucifixion in the same gallery shows a crowded scene of Calvary, but nobody is standing around looking particularly evil or saintly, just dozens of men very busy nailing people to crosses and fetching more nails and timber. Again to the left sits a man by a cross waiting to be crucified, with his head in his hands. I was disconsolate.

On the other hand I was pleased at last to get to see a fresco I've always admired from a distance, Lorenzetti's 'Allegories of Good and Bad Government' in the Palazzo Pubblico in Siena, the first artistic or cultural representation of the ideal of civic society. Unfortunately it is not in terribly good condition so much of the effect is lost. But Siena had everything I'd read about and admired from an historical distance in the way of public architecture and civic space. A magnificent town hall, the great public square outside, and a history of republican and elected local government of a kind going back some 700 years. This was really what I had come to see and feel at first hand – these great early experiments in civil society, in local, self-sustaining political and economic autonomy. All the towns we visited possessed these great public spaces, these histories of self-government, these beautiful public buildings and handsome residential districts and quarters, all enclosed within a fearsome perimeter wall. And that's when the doubts began.

For there was something amiss in the contrast between these astonishing hilltop towns and cities, so self-possessed, so magnificent and filled with buildings, churches, frescoes and paintings, and the ferocious internecine warring between them and within them. There was certainly more blood than paint spilt for most of those 700 years. Within the great Tuscan towns and cities, rich families warred with each other over centuries, recruiting mercenaries and assassins to poison, ambush and massacre each other, kidnap or murder random sons and daughters, husbands and wives, and rape and torture at will. In San Gimignano, which as one approaches across a plain, looms out of the distance as a medieval Manhattan, so many bell towers does it have one bell tower remains known as the *Hungry Tower* – Shelley wrote a poem about it. A family were in residence there one time and a rival family surrounded it, blockaded all the doors and windows, and left everyone inside to starve to death. In Perugia, where the *Palazzo dei Priori* is considered to be one of the greatest architectural achievements of all Italy, the beautiful trefoil windows were also used to throw convicted criminals to their death into the square below. One began to get an inkling that Walter Benjamin was right when he wrote that every product of civilisation is a product of barbarism too. And I remember also, some years before when Larraine and I were camping beside Lago Puccini, visiting Puccini's house and reading an account of his daily duck-shooting expeditions when he often killed more than 200 birds, and finding that the guidebook stated that the great composer could never decide which he preferred most – the piano or the gun.

When the inhabitants weren't murdering each other within each city-state they were busy waging war on all the others. The city-states changed rulers every decade or so after an initial period of peace, perhaps an inevitable aftermath of the appalling chaos which the Black Death brought to Tuscany in the middle of the fourteenth century. In Orvieto, the façade of the Duomo is so beautifully decorated that Pope Leo XIII said that on the Day of Judgement it would float up to heaven carried by its own beauty. But look closely at the exquisitely carved tableaux and what do you see? Sinners being disembowelled, thrown into the flames, roasted on spits. Apparently the town was riven for centuries by bloody vendettas between the principal families, a *grand guignol* drama of arbitrary murder and revenge.

Afternoons at the campsites were spent snoozing and reading, stretched out on a sleeping bag, often in the shade of an olive tree under which I had pitched my tent. There's a certain point about half-way during a trip when one needs a break from the nightly round of socialising, eating and drinking, and intense conversation. What you want is a 'night in'. In Assisi I had such an evening, buying food and wine in the town and enjoying a picnic of my own under the olive tree with *A Life of St Francis of Assisi* . I hadn't until then realised just how important he was to the whole Christian tradition. It was he who denounced all the pomp, hierarchy, labyrinthine organisation and oppressive authority of the church, well before Luther or Calvin, advocating simplicity and austerity in the service of a benign and understanding God. Assisi was full of kitsch trinkets and souvenirs; the T-shirt I would really like to have seen would have said ST FRANCIS SAYS RELAX. In a way the Protestant Reformation has some of its origins in his example, as do all other more gentler versions of the Christian faith, which I admire somewhat as a cultural tradition while believing it to be based on absolute self-delusion. Unfortunately the book was straightforward hagiography. It is difficult to accept that a writer in the 1980s takes as absolute fact that the birds St Francis preached to all listened intently then flew up to kiss his hand. How people can live without understanding the role of metaphor I simply don't know. But that's the nature of religious faith I suppose.

As always you have to go away to hear the gossip about what's happening back at home. Last year I was cycling in Poland when I started talking to another cyclist who told me that our next door neighbour in Stoke Newington was expecting her third baby. The first night in Pisa I got talking to someone from Hackney, who told me about a mutual friend whose funeral he'd attended only a few days before, having been found dead in a flat from a drugs overdose.

A friend once suggested, rather hesitantly, that I had a morbid streak within me: I often wrote about death. It's true, though I don't feel morbid at all. But there is a reason. It all goes back to a particular period between the end of 1978 and the end of 1979 when I went to nine funerals in less than twelve months. This dark period began with the death of Larraine's father, followed shortly after by the death in a house fire of the young black writer Vivian

Usherwood whom I had taught and befriended, and whose poetry I had first published, and who, according to witnesses, was last seen alive hammering on the sealed, double-glazed windows of his flat, engulfed in flames, screaming. A few weeks later came the lonely and rain-swept funeral of an older family friend, a shop steward at Ford's who had been broken by the management, and whose later years were awash with drink. Then, most shockingly, Blair Peach's murder – the sudden disappearance from my life of a friend I really loved. Three months later one of Blair's best friends committed suicide, totally in despair, and I was asked to conduct the funeral, once again at Manor House Cemetery: a younger brother wired up a giant PA system to play Pink Floyd's 'Wish You Were Here'. Then an elderly Hackney man whose autobiography I'd taped, and stayed in touch with, died, then another relative, then another friend's suicide: a talented writer who jumped from the ninth floor of a tower block in Shoreditch. There were others that year. I felt tempted to buy a season ticket out to Manor Park Cemetery. In addition to the trauma of the funerals were the many inquests, in which one sat through the most graphic descriptions of pathological evidence as well as statements by witnesses, police officers and other parties mostly relating to the last hours or minutes of the deceased person's life, the particular fragility of their skull at the point of the blow, the flushed face which gives the most obvious clue to carbon monoxide poisoning, the eye-witness account of your friend climbing over the balcony, and hanging on just for a few seconds before letting go. In the middle of it all we went to France for a holiday and on the motorway heading south our car burst two tyres simultaneously. We rolled over half a dozen times on the motorway, skidded along on the roof for about two hundred yards in fast and heavy traffic, and ended up upside down on the verge – yards short of a large steel motorway sign which would have delivered the *coup de grace.* The car was a write-off and we had bruises and burns from the seat belts, but we were very lucky to have escaped without all being killed. It was not a good summer.

At times that year I dared hardly lift my head in apprehension of another death and another funeral. If it takes a year, as they say, to come to terms with a close bereavement, this chapter of accidents and calendar of deaths took me about three years of feeling empty inside, a walking automaton. This period tempered me once and for all – I quietened down, grew up, and became the more reflective person who writes long letters. It wasn't always like that. But I do know quite a lot about death – which is mostly very cheering in the effects it produces when you've absorbed the lessons. But morbid, no. These experiences also predisposed me to a more detached, quietist view of life, hence my genuine interest in reading about religion.

In one campsite the trees were full of nightingales – the first I've ever heard – and they trilled, sang, improvised, and modulated all night long. Most of the campsites were also alive with fireflies, and late at night walking back to one's tent from the bar or restaurant, the dark lanes and fields would be spectacularly twinkling with lights like an evening walk in a minor seaside resort with illuminations. Snakes too we saw squashed on the road, but I also saw one close to, about two feet long, bright green, in a hedge as I was walking along a small lane into Assisi. More bizarrely, in the fields, particularly where there were cherry trees, you would see giant teddy bears or pandas tied to the upper branches acting as scarecrows, a sort of martyrdom of the fluffy toys.

By the time we arrived in Florence the weather was hopelessly hot, humid and oppressive. Even to stand up and walk to the water tap brought on a flood of perspiration and stickiness. On my first trip into the city, early one morning, I was adroitly robbed by a small gang of boys no older than eleven. It was quite disturbing. Head in the clouds, as always, I suddenly found myself surrounded by children pleading with me to buy some cheap little pamphlets, which I assumed were religious. I declined. They started to grab my arms, beseechingly, then my legs, then pawed my face until I was so alarmed I actually fought back. Too late. Two minutes later I found my wallet was missing from my trouser pocket.

I was hot, I was fed up, I wanted to go home now that the cycling had finished. I wanted movement not stasis. So I climbed the Dome of the Florence Duomo, 465 stairs, of a Piranesi-like, vertiginous narrowness and darkness, mostly between the inner and outer walls of the dome. But the view! When depressed, when agitated, don't stay still, keep moving. It was worth it. And later on that evening four of us found one of those perfect family restaurants, where the food and service were marvellous, and the staff genuinely friendly, and we sat and finally relaxed after the intensity of Florence. A morning in the Uffizi Gallery was worth it, but at times it became impossible to see certain paintings without stepping across the sight-lines of a dozen video cameras or camcorders. They were everywhere; everybody was filming everybody else. Florence was another home movie.

On the other hand, my last image of Florence came at about 2 o'clock in the morning when I crawled out of my tent for a piss and walked by the campsite bar, where all the young students hung out. At that late hour there were still dozens of little groups clustered round tables, all the drink gone, just smoking cigarettes and laughing and talking, and in every group at least one earnest young Dane, Italian, American or Briton strumming an out-of-tune guitar singing 'The Times They Are A Changing' or 'Route 66'. *Plus ça change.*

3 London April 1991

I am often reminded of a letter George Bernard Shaw sent to a friend apologising for writing a long letter as he didn't have time to write a short one. It's a paradox I'm conscious of: that short letters pose insoluble editorial problems of choice and succinctness, whereas longer letters can just let it all hang out, spilling events and news out on to the floor like clothes from the laundry basket, or like papers pulled from a drawer. Life is by nature an untidy mess, stretched and pulled in all directions, discontinuous and haphazard, and therefore trying to describe it is fraught with these problems too – unless you are a miniaturist, polishing aphorisms till they shine. And moods change too – different days, different worlds. And although in the end I believe in the irreducible continuity of the self, almost in a personal teleology, I also know that consciousness changes by the hour. Therefore a long letter becomes a suitcase packed for an unexpected journey, which, disgorged at the end, contains all manner of artefacts, used tickets, cancelled obligations, and other memorabilia.

Over the past decade I reckon I have cycled nearly 20,000 miles – enough to get me to the Andes and back – but most of these miles have been in the form of working journeys in and around central London. Over the years I have had a share in, or the use of, offices at the Elephant and Castle, in Soho, and more recently King's Cross, and I've enjoyed cycling every mile. That's the point about cycling – it's not so much where you go as the sheer range of experience that cycling brings to any journey. For me cycling is, as Wittgenstein (a bicycle owner himself) might have put it, another way of 'being in the world'. It's an intensely physical form of transport, and brings into play nearly all the senses. This makes it the ideal way of travelling in a city like London that is itself kaleidoscopic and in a process of continual change and transformation. A back street route from Hackney to King's Cross can be partly derelict one year and gentrified or radically cosmopolitan the next; the demolition of an old cinema can suddenly transform an urban panorama. Yesterday's office block becomes today's archaeological dig.

The graffiti and fly-posting on the walls and fences keep you constantly in touch with the latest political outrages, community festivals and jazz gigs. The urban street is a living newspaper and the city itself is a form of instant communication: cycling is the best way to read and understand it. I admit that I'm lucky in that, as a freelance writer, I don't have to do the same journey every day, though many of them are fairly regular runs. The longest journeys have taken me through the futuristic landscape of London's docklands, the multi-racial communities and cultures of Southall, Brixton, Brick Lane and Notting Hill, the measured and urbane uniformities of Hampstead Garden Suburb to the bleak wastes of the Greenwich peninsula, abandoned gas works and all. Taxi-drivers have even asked me for directions, assuming often correctly, that the city cyclist knows the minutiae of a city's geography and topography better than most.

Every month or so I change the route and I discover marvellous back streets, terraces and squares, churchyards, cemeteries, canals, tenement buildings and gardens. Recently my route has taken me along Liverpool Road and through Barnsbury, an area dense with eighteenth and nineteenth century squares and terraces, some of them exuding a pre-war air of foreboding in which the spirit of the novelist Patrick Hamilton still prevails; others a renovated and railinged Georgian elegance. But it also takes me past a particular street, with a pub on the corner, which reminds me every time of one of the most interesting people I ever met.

When I was writing about popular literature in the early 1980s I began collecting ACE paperbacks, a garish, tawdry collection of cheap paperbacks which disguised one of the most adventurous and erudite literary lists ever published in Britain. A book reviewer I knew, Nick Kimberley, was also an ACE *aficionado*, and we decided to try to write up the story of ACE publishers and began a search for the man who had started it. A letter to *The Bookseller* produced a couple of leads, including a postcard from Brian Aldiss, which led to a phone call to a number in Hertfordshire where a certain Frank Rudman lived with his ageing mother. The letters we received from our *Bookseller* enquiry spoke in admiring tones about the singular Mr Rudman and his great literary achievement, and so we arranged to meet him. He chose to meet us at an address in Islington, a flat which belonged to one of his friends, a 1940s bohemian setting with gin bottles, manuscripts, ash on the carpet, cats, lorgnette spectacles, a mantelpiece crowded with black and white studio portraits of young matinee idols and glamorous walk-ons, and a lot of velvet and old copies of *The Stage*. Frank Rudman, a small man wearing a trilby and with a cigarette permanently wedged in his mouth, looked like a bookie's runner or a Tally Man. He was friendly but unforthcoming. It was all in the past.

I'm not exaggerating when I say I think he did more for literary culture and intellectual life in post-war Britain than any university department, public cultural body, critical magazine or publisher. He started ACE books in 1949 with £100 demob money and published about 60 titles a year out of a single room in Soho. The books he published often ended up with garish covers displaying exotic foreign women in various states of *déshabillé*, ripped bodices all over the place, lurid covers which dressed some of the most important European and American writing of the twentieth century; his literary tastes were thoroughly experimental and demanding. ACE books were the first to publish in paperback in Britain such writers as Silone, Calvino and all the Italian neo-realists; he published Salinger, Bellow, Mailer, Richard Wright, many Irish writers, as well as novels by Lawrence, Woolf, and many others. He even published William Burroughs' *Junkie*. And he did it mostly standing at the saloon bar with a pint, a fag in his mouth, and the print-run costings on the back of a betting slip. (Plus the latest Moravia, Pavese or Mary McCarthy in his coat pocket to read and decide upon between opening times.)

After about 20 minutes of circular conversation he insisted we come down the pub as it was now opening time – it was about eleven in the morning – where he stood for an hour chirpingly reminiscing over pints of bitter while Nick and I drank orange juice. He must have thought we were two Christian Scientists. A couple of years ago I read his obituary; he remains one of my heroes. When you think of all the hype of publishing today, the expensive offices, the mammoth advances for famous writers, the endless take-overs and machinations in the accountancy department, it is salutary to think of the wiry little man in a trilby with some of the world's greatest literature in manuscript or translation in his shabby raincoat pocket. He had an unerring eye for serious and challenging writing. And every time I cycle past that dowdy corner pub I think of him.

Only six minutes away from elegant Barnsbury, one drops down into Somers Town and the back of King's Cross where the flats appear burnt out, the young prostitutes and the junkies hang out around the pubs and cafes, the children are poorly dressed and shod, there's dogshit and mangy alsations on the streets, and smashed cars. Since the bad winter the scene has been further depressed by the continuing deterioration of the roads, some of which now have pot-holes a foot deep, giving the area the appearance of a city recently strafed or bombed. Nothing could ever make me love this area; the only animation it gets is every Friday when a street market is held in Chalton Street, and the Asian stall-holders set up clothes stalls alongside the British stall-holders selling soft drinks, soup mixes, packets of biscuits and cakes and shrink-wrapped meat pies all past their sell-by dates. I cannot find any redeeming features.

But when I'm on my bike I am always happy. The streets and parks fly past me. The daffodils are now out in the gardens and window boxes, the blackbirds are tuning up in the flowering cherry trees which are already coming into bloom, and every day there's something new. Yesterday I noticed for the first time a row of old large houses which each had steps going up to the front door flanked by balustrade walls on which there were giant obelisks and sphinxes. Inlaid into the obelisk, two to a house, a dozen houses in a row, was the word NILE. Perhaps the houses had been built by a dedicated Egyptologist or Mason steeped in cabbalistic knowledge.

These days, though, I'm often on an Inter-City train going to or returning from somewhere, and reading Enzensberger, Kapuściński, or some of the other Granta-published documentary writers, or the *Collected W.H. Auden* in a hotel bedroom. Nowadays I actually recognise some of the buffet car staff on the Swansea train or the Manchester run, and they recognise me. Or I think I do. For I'm am beginning to develop a strange habit of thinking that I recognise everybody wherever I go. I sit on a train and think, 'I'm sure I know him, or her.' Is the world so small or am I entering a twilight world of permanent *déjà vu*?

Mostly train journeys are bliss. I am completely alone and unable to be interrupted; I work and read intently. I look out on to the Cleveland Hills, the Pennines, or the coastal hills surrounding Port Talbot, watching the sheep crawling over the heather like grubs on a carcass, or the clouds skimming the hills, and the sun breaking through onto the downs below. I am always impressed how in the open stretches the wind has over time flattened the hedges or how a whole copse or forest has developed the same sloping angle away from the prevailing wind. Occasionally there is a nightmare. The following piece comes straight from my notebook:

> This morning I was travelling out to Southend from Liverpool Street on an almost empty commuter train when someone threw themselves under the wheels at Brentwood Station. I didn't see anything, but I was up at the front of the train near the driver when he sounded his horn and then we seemed to hit a pile of sand – it was exactly like ploughing through shingle or sand for about ten seconds. The train rapidly slowed to a halt and we waited in a stretch of woodland for about 20 minutes while nothing happened. It began to snow, other trains passed us by, people walked their dogs in the woods. The train then continued to the next station. I didn't realise what had happened until a woman came walking down the train, ashen-faced, and told me. She'd asked the ticket collector.
>
> At Shenfield we were all asked to leave the train and wait for the one behind. I was anxious about being late for a meeting, but I was also beginning to feel a bit spaced out. As we left the train it was impossible not to notice some smears of blood on the metalwork. It was a low, low morning under a grey Essex sky, with a very cold easterly wind and flurries of driving snow. I hadn't had breakfast and my mouth tasted of cardboard and my stomach seemed filled with ash.
>
> On the way back, only a couple of hours later, I was undecided about whether consciously to look out for the spot where the accident had happened. Yet I wanted the thing confirmed and abetted by evidence of some kind. Few people can avert their eyes from disaster, or like Orpheus not look back. But by then snow covered everything.
>
> Shortly after the train passed Brentwood Station again, we came into a stretch of Essex suburbia with high embankments along the track, part-covered with nettles and bushes thinned by winter, and there walking nonchalantly along the ridge was the most beautiful red fox I have ever seen. It belonged to another world. I almost shouted to the other passengers but already the train had passed on. The sudden sight of this brilliant creature lightened my apprehensions

and morbid mood. It was as if as one life had been extinguished, some kind of transmigration had occurred, and another had risen from the flames.

Shortly I will be working in Bolton on and off for about six weeks, and I'm really looking forward to that. I've been there twice now and it is a town on its own. It has the finest Victorian neo-classical town hall in Britain, a building worthy of Athens, overlooking a stunning open square. Bolton is very consciously self-contained and rooted. I had afternoon tea with one of the councillors in the Members' Tea Room. 'Been to Bolton, before, have you? No place like it, though I say it myself as one born and bred. We're very prudent people, us Boltonians, we don't like extremes, if you get my meaning, nothing too adventurous but on the other hand nothing totally dull. It's the Protestant tradition, and more recently Methodism. Did you know we're having the Methodist Conference in Bolton this year. Naturally we were on Cromwell's side in the Civil War.' 'Naturally', I replied. 'Ah but Wigan! Don't talk to me about Wigan. Spend money like water Wigan people do. Nightclubs, big cars, supported the Royalist cause in 1666 too.' 'Did they, oh dear'. 'No, Bolton is Bolton.' 'Exactly how far away is Wigan?' I asked 'Nearly seven miles.'

All towns are *sui generis* – standard solutions or *prêt-à-porter* analyses never fit. You have to get under the skin. You have to sit in the hotel bar after closing time to pick up the nuances and the gossip, or have lunch in department store restaurants where respectable middle-aged couples tell another story. I've also developed a knack of ferreting out the hidden spaces in town where the subcultures meet. I can usually identify the pub where drugs change hands by my second visit. In Bedford I recently discovered a coffee shop above a furniture department store where not only did the middle classes meet but also the young gay male shop assistants and estate agent clerks, a homely, slightly camp space in between the three-piece suites and Dralon curtains, much more pleasant and amenable than a fast food bar or noisy pub.

I enjoy my work. I'm only ever away perhaps one night a fortnight; it's not something I'm that keen on, though I'm getting better at instantly judging small hotels from the outside. In Bolton recently I'd been wrongly booked and the place I was to stay in was full. They put me in a taxi and sent me over to another guest house where I stood on the doorstep for ten minutes hammering and ringing the bell. Eventually a guest let me in. It transpired that the amiable ex-trade union officer who ran this place was completely deaf, a rather awkward handicap for someone whose livelihood depends on unexpected people ringing or knocking at the door. While he was getting me to write my name in the guest book the front door bell rang again but he didn't hear a thing. 'I think someone's at the door,' I said. 'Sorry?' he said.

They are mostly men in these hotels and guest houses, 'on the road' in a way Kerouac never imagined. They roughly fall into two types: the younger lads working for British Telecom as fitters or engineers, who dress in jeans and stick closely together, and the middle-aged men in double breasted suits, striped shirts and white collars, very much on their own, working the territory as commercial salesmen. The younger ones avoid us middle-aged men like the plague, as if our age was catching. As if they might go to bed one night in Room 17 as a brash 24 year old with Brut aftershave and wake up in the morning 45 years old with a beer belly and a bad back. Because every room has a television set, it's the only time I ever see the *Late Show* or documentaries about city brokers who gave it all up to run a small hotel in the Orkneys, or policemen who found religion.

Another thing I was struck by in Bolton was the self-assurance and exuberance of the older working-class women, often to be seen in town in large groups or gangs. Because it was a mill town, women have worked collectively there for over a hundred years. It shows. I talked to the Director of the Bolton Octagon Theatre – both shows I've seen there have been marvellous productions – and he says the backbone of the theatre audience in Bolton is exactly these intelligent, well-dressed and self-assured women. They attend in groups and make forthright pronouncements on the plays in the interval and in the bar after. They know what a good night out is, and they meet everybody else in town – theatre types, London arts consultants, shop managers and policemen – as equals. It's impressive.

For a while I also worked part-time for the Labour Party at the House of Commons as a policy adviser. I used to draft articles and policy statements and even substantially helped draft Labour's Arts Policy for the 1987 election. Oh, the infantile delusions of power, writing sentences that began, 'Under a Labour

Government we will ensure that professional dance will be available to all regions...', or 'We will re-organise all the Regional Arts Associations from top to bottom...' Words, words, words. Working in and around Parliament was like holidaying in Beirut. Everybody works in indescribably cramped and archaic conditions, the phones ring all the time, party hacks and *apparatchiks* scrap speeches, completely re-word press releases, embargo the most innocent of ideas, pull rank, stab in the back, out-manoeuvre, outflank, destroy by rumour and innuendo, and generally ensure that what was a good idea at nine in the morning is completely scribbled all over, trodden underfoot, screwed up and in the waste bin by four in the afternoon. I realised that life is too short to spend time cycling to Westminster and so I quit. I still write stuff on a voluntary basis and call in for chat from time to time, but it was hopeless. Other lives, other cycle paths. I had started with high hopes, and probably a big head, but it ended in tears.

Last night my (now) old friend Dagmar sat in our kitchen talking to me about post-modernism. Dagmar is in her late sixties and is over here from the former GDR for a fortnight, attending conferences, reading in the British Museum, that sort of thing. She has just left the Communist Party after a lifetime. She is a tough, dissident, communist intellectual who now says unemotionally that everything she ever believed in to do with her country (the old East Germany) has been destroyed. She was a real base/superstructure East European marxist. Now she believes in feminism and holds weekly discussion groups in her kitchen for younger women at the university from which she has been sacked in disgrace. She wrote a letter and publicly distributed it denouncing the new administration as time-servers, and no better than the Stalinists she'd fought before them. But post-modernism? 'Yes, Ken, there is something in it. We should question everything, all the old hierarchies of value. Of course it doesn't mean we have to float in a world of complete relativity of all things – no, obviously some things are more important than others – but we must question everything now. That is good. You know I now question the Enlightenment; as a German I was led to believe that was the most important thing in history ever. But it isn't. Why is so called rational man a more important person than a medieval peasant? I used to believe in continuity. Now I don't. There is no immanent meaning to anything.'

I drove her back to the flat in Finchley where she stays with an elderly relative who came here during the war. 'You know already I am looking forward to going back. Isn't that strange? That damned country is like a drug. After a fortnight away I want to get back, with all its misery. That's not rational is it? Shouldn't we also question these deeper feelings as well?'

Yet even an out-of-the-blue invitation to undertake a lecture tour in Australia which came the other day could not shake off a low mood I've been in for a few days. I don't know why. I can cope with most weather but I get depressed by the wind. Apart from the fact that cycling is murder in a wind, it's just an elemental power that seems uncontrollable and often so destructive. It distorts things – trees, shrubs, fields – and wrecks things. But it's most probably the world political situation, which seems terrible wherever you look. War, starvation, nationalism, riots, communal violence, the break-up of institutions, dissolution, volatile allegiances, the end of ideology of any kind. I talked to Dagmar about this. 'You have to let the storm blow around you,' she said. 'It's important that everything is questioned, and it's important that all our values are challenged. We really must wake up and do some hard thinking. Do you want an easy life? No.'

And just like the occasional book which is genuinely uplifting, so a television programme comes along which unlocks forgotten worlds. A week ago there was a documentary about the lives of Irish labourers in Britain – the men who dig the holes. This is really a long and fascinating part of British social history that is rarely engaged with. For about three years of my life, between 17 and 20, I worked and lived largely in the company of Irish building workers. My first job on leaving school was to work for an Essex civil engineering company as a trainee stores clerk and I did that until I was 20, though for most of the time I worked for a civil engineering company working in Liverpool, Birmingham and Glasgow on very large piling contracts. Three years largely wading through slurry and mud in all weathers, fetching welding rods and oxygen cylinders, shackles, engine parts, setting levels for the men to work to on site, laying out lines for drilling the piles from drawings, fetching the directors from the airport or station. I lived in furnished rooms or lodgings and I spent hundreds of evenings drinking with the men – who were mostly Irish – and I found them wonderful.

They often had characters larger than life because in a way they led singular lives untouched by domesticity, community ties, or sense of place. They were travellers, from site to site, and they fed on legends. Legendary jobs, legendary disasters, and legendary gangers and foremen. They were rarely violent, rarely used sexual innuendoes or told sexual jokes of any kind, but spoke endlessly rather of work, of other men, of lodging houses, and were great raconteurs, great men of 'the crack'. The ability to hold an audience of other men spellbound for half an hour at a time round a pub table was the greatest attribute one could possess. Yet they aged rapidly and saddened with age. Men who looked 60 turned out to be only 40, yet their deeply lined and scarred faces, hands with missing fingers, wheezing chests, and shrunken eyes gave some evidence of the toll taken by rough work in bad conditions, poor diets, and a life without very much personal love or even an occasional gentle touch.

Because I had the Land Rover as part of my job, I would occasionally be asked 'for a good drink, mind' to fetch a young brother or cousin coming over from Ireland for the first time at the airport. I would wait there at the exit door holding a piece of card saying O'Malley or O'Donaghue, until a thin, poorly dressed and totally terrified young man would approach me and say something in an accent so thick that I could only nod. These were 15 and 16 year olds from the hill farms of Donegal, Sligo, Mayo, County Clare, Connemara and Kerry, leaving home for the first time to spend the rest of their lives working on building sites in another country and sending most of the money home. By the end of the one hour flight they were already homesick, and gazed out of the window of the Land Rover as we drove through the suburbs of Birmingham or Glasgow wide-eyed and uneasy. Within a month – and this transformation always shocked me – they had filled out with beer and breakfasts, adopted the standard uniform of boots, corduroy trousers and a suit jacket tied with string, and were telling wild stories along with the rest of them. I still have vivid memories of dozens of them. Occasionally I am reminded of this 'hidden culture' by a notice in a pub window, announcing Irish singers or St Patrick's Day socials. My favourite is still to be seen in a large pub near Finsbury Park where every Sunday you can go and listen to 'Kevin O'Connor – The JCB Man'.

4 London – Venice December 1991

Another dream about punctures. I suppose everybody has to have some symbolic dream symbol for thwarted ambitions, delayed satisfactions, hubris and pride deflated. Not surprisingly, since I cycle almost every day, my frustrated dreams usually involve punctures. I can't get there – wherever there really is, because of unmendable punctures; in real life I can fix them easily, but in my dreams I can't. What I need is Dr Freud's puncture repair kit, the repair kit to beat all others. Alas, it will never exist.

More and more I find the only pleasure in writing is in detail, observation, and truthfulness of description. Trying to describe from memory one of my father's lorries, the smell of the hot engine oil, the cigarette ash, the cracked windscreen, the collection of outdated *Evening News* on the floor, the empty Senior Service packets everywhere and the whiff of Guinness in the feverish air: that is my father to me more than any set of abstracted psychological categories. So instead of writing a diary of grand thoughts, what the French I recently discovered describe as *les longs espoirs et les vastes pensées*, I simply try to describe the physical world as I see it.

The best thing which happened to us recently arose quite unexpectedly. We got invited to a wedding. Out of the blue, an invitation came through the post inviting us to the wedding in the local synagogue of an occasional friend and political ally of ours for over 20 years, a long-haired, bearded, ageing hippy/trotskyist who taught both Ben and Anna in primary school and who – although we've known him for a long time – we have always kept a discreet distance from because of his over-zealousness. He was going back to his Jewish roots, he told us, the last time we met him in the High Street, a Safeways plastic bag full of leaflets in one hand and a baby in a buggy in the other. At the time we didn't realise this meant getting married to the young woman he was living with and with whom he'd recently had the delightful, gurgling baby.

We'd been around at the time of his first child, nearly 16 years ago, when he and his then partner were homeless after she came out of hospital with the three day old. We put them up for about ten days while they found accommodation. On the last evening with us he got drunk and denounced us for our bourgeois life style. We have – and always have had – contradictory feelings about Bernie: admiration for his tireless campaigning and endless proselytising, at the same time as keeping a wary distance in fear of being found wanting in revolutionary zeal. Bernie was a three-meetings-a-night person. He was also a fine, if disorganised, teacher, and Ben and Anna both really enjoyed their year with him in the temporary hut to which he was naturally banished by a succession of disapproving head-teachers. Bernie always taught in the hut. He was also adored by many of the Turkish and West Indian parents, school-helpers and cleaning ladies, on whose behalf, and their children's, he campaigned again and again. On any anti-racist or anti-deportation demonstration, Bernie would always be there with the school banner surrounded by parents and helpers whom he'd cajoled and inspired into coming out on the streets. You need a certain kind of nerve to be so unembarrassedly political like that; I don't have it and neither does Larraine really, though she's more publicly demonstrative than me.

So it's a rather damp, blowy night in the leafy northern borders of Stoke Newington, outside the Progressive Synagogue in Amhurst Park. We're bemused by the whole idea. But we've wrapped a present, scribbled a greeting on yet another tasteful arthouse card, put our best clothes on and crossed the road dodging the 253 buses and the Safeways traffic, prepared for anything. Inside, the synagogue is crowded with people of all colours, shapes and sizes. It's a carnival in fact. Yamulkas for all the men, but the women able to enter with bare heads. The last 20 years come flooding back to us in the form of familiar faces grown greyer, more lined, thinner or fatter, happier or drawn. Wild-haired young women Communist Party activists who commandeered the local nursery campaigns in the early 1970s are now middle-aged matriarchs; angst-ridden young Jewish adolescents I taught at Hackney Downs School are balding, plump solicitors. The babies and toddlers who attended Larraine's playgroup or nursery are glamorous and handsome teenagers. It's fine. But how we have all moved back into the mainstream of life again. For down the aisle carrying the giant *havdala* candles, escorting Bernie and his mum and uncle, come two good friends last seen with *Smash the Fascists!* banners in their hands – and now in iridescent mohair suits. And looking suitably serious and even reverent, their *ouvrierist* donkey coats and Dr Martens cherry-reds safely at home no doubt.

The ceremony is as delightful as it is unexpected. Bernie and his wife-to-be have produced (good teachers as always) an information sheet about the wedding, giving order of service, the meaning of the most important Jewish words, and a short explanation of the various rituals. The whole ceremony takes place under a canopy, the *chupah*, which symbolises, as the young, slightly giggly, woman rabbi explains, the Garden of Eden where we can all be happy or return to, if only for a moment. For this short ceremony, we are in the Garden of Eden again, as so many millions of believers have been before, even if just for one blissful moment in their lives. A young woman violinist plays a jerky, rather atonal, folk song while everybody's finding their place; this turns out to have been written by Bernie when he was twelve for his grandmother. (Bernie is also a fairly accomplished musician and painter.) Unlike the standard Church of England service with its fixed geographies and hierarchies of place, everybody's up on stage, half in, half out of the chupah: parents, brothers and sisters, children, friends, and it feels more like the end of a Gary Glitter Christmas Concert than a formal wedding. There's a choir behind us in a gallery. Most of the service is sung by the cantor, in between him laughing and smiling at the whole world. Po-faced and pompous this is not. The bride has a garland of flowers in her hair, a crown of giant daisies it looks like to me. The Turkish and West Indian women in the congregation are in floods of smiling tears, and even the spiky-haired last-ditch trotskyist cadres, few that there are, are suitably impressed by it all.

I suspect Bernie has rigged this particular service, as it seems to contain bits and pieces from various progressive, orthodox and even anachronistic services and rituals. At the height of the ceremony Myra, Bernie's wife-to-be, circles Bernie seven times slightly flushed with embarrassment; there is a glass of wine, an exchange of rings which naturally Bernie has mislaid, some very solemn vows according to the laws of Moses. Bernie and Myra are then engulfed and wrapped almost completely in a large prayer shawl, and then seven friends make a blessing each. Another glass of wine, a shouted *Mazeltov*!, and the glass is hurled to the floor by Bernie – and bounces upright unbroken. It is then stamped underfoot. The giggling rabbi tells us that the marriage should last until such time as the glass is restored to its unbroken state again. The register is signed and everybody files out in procession after Bernie, Myra and Bernie's mother – who I used to know when her husband was still alive and now is palpably more shocked by Bernie's embracing of respectability than she has been by anything Bernie has got up to before. She is beaming. That over, the invitees can now get back to the serious business of recognising each other from all those years ago, trying to match partners and children to old faces, noting who has aged less flatteringly than oneself, and so on. What else are weddings for?

The ceremony over, we all trooped downstairs to a large hall beneath the synagogue where tables had been laid for nearly two hundred. There was a genuine Jewish klezmer band who played raucous, jolly, occasionally manic folk tunes, airs and dances continuously for the rest of the evening. There was champagne brought to the tables all night long, a free bar serving every kind of drink imaginable, and food – smoked salmon, gefilte fish, gherkins, coleslaw, beigels, cheesecake – for everyone. This really was a celebration. The atmosphere didn't quieten for a second all night long: the room was buzzing with loud chatter, jokes, laughter, children shouting or dancing in the cloakroom to a borrowed portable tape-recorder. People moved from table to table recognising old friends or making it up with old adversaries. It really was an evening of making amends, renewing lost friendships, coming to terms with the people we had become one generation on. It was enchanting: outside a wet Tuesday night in gloomy autumnal North Hackney, inside a fairy-tale wedding.

There were speeches of course. I think that public speeches on occasions like these can be among the most marvellous pieces of theatre or public culture. There was one speech that held the complete hall captivated for perhaps ten minutes, which created a silence, attentiveness and rapt, willed involvement so that you could, as they say, have heard a pin drop. It was given by a sacked Nottinghamshire miner who had been befriended by Bernie during the strike, and who had established quite deep friendships with some Stoke Newington teachers. His deceptively artless ability to move in tone and register from jokes about Bernie's haircut to a peroration on the meaning of the word community, back to witty asides about trendy lefties in London who wouldn't know a pit prop from a parking meter, and then on to a state of the nation commentary, changing register yet again and finally to a soliloquy on the uses and meanings of words like love and history, had us all entranced. But over the years I have heard other speeches – at weddings, funerals, in draughty halls, on rainswept public platforms – which I would not exchange for anything spoken on stage at the National Theatre, in Parliament, or from the lectern of an inaugural professorial address. It is interesting that in one of my own favourite moments on film – the baptism dinner speech in Bergman's *Fanny and Alexander* – the evocation of 'this little world' of the theatre, is actually made flesh in the slightly larger world of a family celebration. Larraine and I weren't quite the last to leave – though originally we had made plans to be among the first – and we went home singing.

* * *

All of a sudden the weather has changed. It is that time of year when the geraniums are brought in from the garden; already we've had a couple of early morning frosts. After the winds of the last week the lawn is covered in hard inedible pears, leaves, twigs and conkers. There are spiders, and spiders' webs, everywhere. This coming Saturday I shall meet up with old friends from past cycling trips for the last cycle ride of the year: a train from London Bridge to Frant in Kent, a 45 mile ride through the orchards, the beech forests and the chalk commons, stopping at Sissinghurst Castle for tea, then back to London and a couple of pints at The George in Southwark. Last year it was shorts and T shirt weather, the year before it was Force 9 gales and driving rain. But as Ted Hughes once said, there's no such thing as bad weather, only inappropriate clothing. Well he would, wouldn't he? But then as Terry Eagleton said about Ted Hughes, it's a pity he's run out of animals.

Ben was 22 earlier this week. I have to admit I never thought I'd be buying him a 500-page biography of Wittgenstein for his birthday, which I knew he was keen to read. Six years ago I would have been surprised if he had been able to get a job in Woolworth's. Never be surprised at the way children and young people change, or transform themselves; that's one of the lessons I've actually learnt from life. Anna left home a couple of months ago and is sharing a flat with two friends about a quarter of a mile away and enjoying her independence though missing the ready-cooked meals, the stocked fridge, the central heating, the free newspapers, the free laundry, and so on. The difference in her relationship with us in that short time has been remarkable. She is suddenly so much more confident, adult, at ease with us; she calls by two or three times a week, kisses us both on the cheek when she comes in, sits down in the kitchen like an old friend, drinks tea and tells us her news. It's great. One of her fellow students goes to evening class with his portable telephone, just in case someone rings up with details of the latest warehouse party that he is involved in organising. I'm not sure I can take much more of the enterprise culture. Or is it envy?

Naming the emotion or event correctly is the aim of all good writing. I taught some European colleagues a new word recently, although their English was mostly excellent. The word was 'junket'. Despite having little work at present in Britain, I'm increasingly being invited to lecture abroad. Just four weeks ago a fax pinged out of the machine at the office where I work part-time asking if, at short notice, Franco, Charles and I could speak at a conference in Trento, near Venice. Naturally we went, though separately. The trip gave us two days in the mountains of the Italian Tyrol at Trento University, and one and a half days in Venice, all expenses paid. I was rather taken aback at the sheer indulgence of it all. For it transpired that the conference was a hastily put together job to put a particular university department on the map in the eyes of a particular Christian Democrat politician who needs some spare copy for his political CV. It was, in fact, principally organised to get two column inches in the Italian specialist press linking the name of the politician with an international cultural event! No expense was spared.

Venice was astonishing: everybody says it, and everybody has to say it again. The best way to approach it is by boat from the airport, cutting a swathe through the open seas. We were there in a very damp, drizzly, dark November, but nothing could take away the aura of the place. Part fantasy, part nightmare, the labyrinth of tiny canals, alleys, bridges, tenement buildings never seems to end. It is worth remembering that Calvino's finest book, *Invisible Cities,* is really a reverie on the multiple archaeologies and architectures of Venice. The inside of St Mark's reminded me of the interiors in Eisenstein's films about Ivan the Terrible, dark, vaulted, gothic interiors, echoing and bloodied by devotional madness. Charles and I spent an evening wandering round the myriad alleys of the old Jewish quarter, the first Jewish ghetto in European history. The Venetian obsession with casinos, balls and the wearing of masks is horribly real. The whole place is pretty unnerving. Not a place to have a breakdown in I think.

Place and the sense of place is becoming an obsession. Our friend Ann in Wales recently sent us a wonderful letter, largely about going back to Greenham Common ten years after the first march arrived there, which she had been instrumental in organising and which had started from Wales. She described the many levels of meaning and possible interpretations that accrue to places; the contradictory emotions aroused by the gorse and hawthorn common land, the military presence, the feelings of sisterhood with other women, allied to a knowledge of the many motives people have for leaving home in the name of politics, and for always being somewhere else. Even in the worst times, lots of things can be solved by keeping on the move. Brecht caught this emotion in one of his poems, when he described himself standing by the roadside, as a wheel was changed on the car in which he was escaping from Germany, hating where he had been, hating where he was going, and yet impatient to be standing still.

Time goes so much faster when life is fairly routine. In contrast, although experiences rush past one, more of them, endlessly new and different when one is on the move, the end result is that time seems stretched and fuller. My four day trip to Venice and Trento was full of incident and detail – missed late night trains at unknown stations in the Dolomite mountains, snow falling outside the buffet bar; a ferry ride between the islands in Venice but on the open sea with the Saturday night casino crowd; a crowded restaurant in Trento talking about what useful bits and pieces can be retrieved and recycled from the wreck of marxism-leninism; reading Larraine's mad Jewish aunt's copy of Byron on the plane, the pages marked by 1950s betting slips, an admirable juxtaposition of the sacred and profane that I like to live my own life by. What we are seeking in travel, says the critic Paul Fussell, is anomaly. We are also seeking the temporary victory of distance (and experience) over time.

Hard frosts, now, but brilliant blue skies, and how fabulous it is to cycle through the winter streets of Bloomsbury, Clerkenwell, the Angel, Highbury and Stoke Newington, especially at dusk as the lights come on. This way of life suits me; I don't want things to change. And yet I do. I want always to be on the move, and yet I deeply feel the need for settlement and the respite of home. Last night, while Larraine and I were sitting in the kitchen eating supper, we heard for the first time for nearly a year, the blood-curdling call of an owl in the small copse at the bottom of our garden. That eerie, echoing cry, must have penetrated every kitchen, bedroom, hall, flat or house within a quarter of a mile. Nothing drowns it out, it insinuates into every spare inch of space, chilling and unnerving: and it knits all of these streets and houses together, if only for a while.

5 Santander – Oporto September 1987

As so often, it starts in a bike shop. I have become the sort of person who needs to breathe the air of rubber inner tubes, puncture glue and aerosol lubricant every so often in a favourite bike shop; to stand around and chat bike talk with other *aficionados* while the hours melt away. Shop talk in other words. Where nineteenth century radicalism was supposed to have been promulgated in shoe-makers' work-rooms, in barbers' shops and in newspaper composing rooms, then late twentieth century radical politics (including its feminist and ecological strands) seems increasingly to be sited in bicycle shops. That's where the pamphlets are now to be found, the noticeboards and contact lists, and where word is often spread about the next anti-road campaign or civil liberties demonstration.

The big retail chains have already appropriated the alternative health food business, and feminist and radical bookselling, but I can't see them ever wanting to sell – and more importantly repair – bikes. (It is not a constituent part of the new retailing imperative to actually repair things, and so I believe bicycle shops are at least safe for a while from the predatory chains.) And this is where once a year now I thumb through the holiday brochures – a handful of rather earnest pamphlets on recycled paper giving mileages, starting and finishing points, and prices, accompanied by ink drawings of people on bicycles freewheeling along rolling chalk downs with smiles as fixed as those on the faces of Soviet Young Pioneers. The illustrations are by the kind of people who usually draw wild herbs in vegan cookery books. There's usually a windmill in there somewhere, or a timbered pub.

One itinerary leapt off the page: a fourteen day, five hundred mile ride along the north coast of Spain and down into Portugal, starting at Santander and finishing up in Oporto. Now I've never been to Spain, mostly because for many years it was considered out of bounds to radicals whilst Franco was still in power. Yet I've always wanted to go, largely because I've always believed that the interior and north-west coast of Spain remains amongst the most unchanged – and even uncharted – terrain in Europe today. In fact when I went to Stanford's Map Shop in Long Acre, a wonderful shop that could feature in a short story by Chatwin or Borges, the only maps available of large parts of Galicia and Andalusia are the 1:100,000 military maps published by the Cartografia Militar de Espana. Visiting Portugal in the same holiday seemed an added bonus.

There were sixteen cyclists on the trip, and with the exception of one American and two computer programmers from Oxfordshire, I knew somebody whom every one of the other thirteen knew too. Small world: our mutual friends. But if, as it most certainly seems, London is now the centre of radical cycling, then Finsbury Park appears the epicentre. One could surmise that in the absence of movement at home – in life, in politics – people seek it by travelling abroad, in cases such as this through considerable physical exertion and a concomitant loss, if only temporary, of a restless, enervating urban self. Shiva Naipaul once wrote that, 'All journeys begin the same way. All travel is a form of self-extinction.'

According to our printed instructions, on leaving the ferry at Santander, we would find the crew vehicles on the quay: namely, one beaten up ex-British Telecom 35 cwt van painted yellow with the hallucinatory company logo hand-painted on the side, as if by a spider tied to a paint brush; one caravan towed behind (weighed down to the axles with muesli we later discovered) which had probably seen better days on a by-pass on the Southend Arterial Road selling teas and burgers and racing tips; one three-wheeled Reliant car; and one Volvo estate with bike racks on the roof. This support team had already brought one tour to a finish in Santander, and were now embarked on the second leg.

The male crew were spirited and amiable, and the women friendly and informal. But as they waited for us, they were also waiting for the main organiser, the mind and intellect behind the tour, who had apparently gone looking for a bank more than a half an hour previously and still hadn't returned. Nothing could happen without him. And then he arrived, this already mythical figure, and he came in style. Straw panama hat, cigar, tanned, good looking with the boyish looks of a Peter O'Toole – and slightly swaying. This was Ashbury. It was like the first appearance of Lee Marvin in *Cat Ballou*, of Albert Finney in *Under the Volcano* or of Jack Nicholson in *Easy Rider*. It was a portent either of great things, or disaster.

Along with most of the others I quickly grew quite fond of Ashbury – there wasn't the tiniest shred of malevolence or bad faith in him at all – but at times he could be overwhelming by virtue of the power of his personality and the intensity of his occasionally drunken hippie angst. Ashbury, like the roads we travelled over the next fortnight, was down and up, up and down, all of the time. He rolled cigarettes the size of toilet rolls and smoked them constantly. He was always laughing, but with one of those slightly chesty apoplectic laughs that sounded like a starter motor unconnected to a proper engine, and which once started could not be stopped. Sometimes the sweat poured from him when he was simply standing still or sitting down. He was the centre of attention whenever he was around because of his endless stream of anecdotes, exhortations, denunciations, jokes, philosophising – and, if we happened to be in a bar, orders for more drinks.

The routine was that every day, after breakfast, the cyclists would pack their tents and load their luggage into the van and then set off for the next evening's campsite, whilst the crew cleared up the site, shopped for food and then drove on ahead to pitch camp and prepare tea and supper at the next site. They travelled as a convoy, except for the Volvo which followed up behind the cyclists in case one of the bikes broke down or one of the cyclists' legs gave up. Occasionally we would arrive at the next site ahead of the crew and would be there to watch the effect on the campsite as this tatty wagon train rolled off the road and pulled into the camp. Respectable paterfamilias, grown men and women, couples sitting in deckchairs outside their ornate family tents enjoying an aperitif, stared in amazement and horror, clearly hoping that this battered caravanserai wouldn't come to rest and pitch next to them. Children stood up from their games on the grass to come and stare in disbelief or giggle; the three-wheeler always drew an incredulous crowd of adults and children, poking and bumping to see if it was for real or not. But Ashbury had yet another treat in store for them. For if he happened to be driving the luggage van, then as soon as he got into camp he would turn on the sound system to clear his head. The most valuable thing in the old Telecom van – as valuable as the van itself most likely – was a cassette deck and amplifier attached to two enormous Wharfdale speakers welded to the inside of the van, which also had considerable amplifying powers of its own. No sooner had the handbrake been applied and Ashbury had rolled another cigarette, then across the campsite would blast Talking Heads, Van Morrison, Miles Davis, John Prine, Ted Hawkins, or some 1960s West Coast surfing compilation, and Ashbury would come alive again, boogieing his way to the camp toilets, hurling luggage out of the van onto the grass, or pulling a broken chainset or bottom bracket to pieces with his bare hands while he sang along. He was at his happiest when, dressed in overalls, hands covered in grease, he stood at his work bench mending a bike, a hand-rolled cigarette in his mouth and a beer bottle at his right hand. (For it was beer in the day, wine in the early evening, and spirits after dark.)

For the first four days we were cycling in the Asturias. We simply left Santander and cycled west, keeping the Atlantic on our right, until we came into Portugal. The route had been designed to keep us off the main roads – such as there were – and on tiny lanes criss-crossing the hills and mountains that follow the coast all along. This meant, basically, leaving a coastal camp site each morning, climbing a hill range heading inland, and in the late afternoon following a river valley down back again to the coast and another campsite. The weather was continuously almost perfect – early morning mist clearing by mid-morning to reveal a powder blue sky and a warm bright sun. In fourteen days we had just the one torrential afternoon shower.

The 'Costa Verde' reminded me of Cornwall or the Pembrokeshire coast, with the additional bonus of fine, hot, cloudless weather. Inland we cycled through woods of eucalyptus trees and oaks and other broad-leaf trees, which thinned out on the highest of the hills to become gorse and heather moorland. We rarely encountered any large towns at all, but cycled along empty lanes which threaded together a large number of tiny hamlets and villages along the way. The further west we cycled, the poorer the people were. When we started, the most common form of transport we noticed was the donkey cart; later in Galicia we found it not uncommon to see carts pulled by milking cows; in Portugal women and children went barefoot to the fields and carried enormous burdens on their backs and on their heads.

I usually cycled on my own. Quite often I would pull off the road and find a field to stretch out in, to rest, swig water, and feast on fruit and dried nuts. It is impossible to describe quite how teeming this landscape was – with butterflies, moths, cicadas, beetles, caterpillars and other small insects. All kinds of grasses, shrubs and wildflowers were evident in profusion. Each square foot of grass seemed to be alive with movement, uncontaminated by insecticides, chemicals or other kinds of environmental pollution, and one realised just how fecund and teeming nature can be. I have never seen anything like this richness and profusion of the natural habitat in Britain, where increasingly the fields and hedgerows are devoid of all diversity. In natural and uncontaminated landscapes, the world does not grow smaller but rather extends itself in microscopic detail, a shifting world mirroring that of quantum physics, chaos theory, indeterminacy and fissipariousness. The American naturalist writer, Annie Dillard, has described this best, most notably in her wonderful book, *Tinker's Creek.*

In the Asturias everybody was busy cutting the clover fields which surrounded their cottages and houses, and loading it all on to donkey carts to be stored for the winter. Even the smartest of the houses was surrounded not by a decorative garden but by a clover field, which both men and women scythed and stacked and then carted. So every morning we found ourselves cycling past men and women walking along the lanes with great scythes on their shoulders, the steel blades glinting in the sun; we gave them a wide berth. I can also say that I really did hear genuine folk-singing in the fields on several occasions: most usually a man on his own sharpening a scythe or loading the donkey cart, but singing a very strange – to my ears quite atonal – song. We all commented on the fact that in the whole of our ride we saw no evidence at all of any form of industrial agriculture, nor, amazingly, any sign of a wheat, corn or any other kind of cereal crop. Sweetcorn, yes, small vegetable plots, yes; but no cash crops of any kind. No sheep either, just goats, single milking cows and donkeys. It was not uncommon to see a man or a woman standing alone in their small field grazing their only cow, holding on to it by a rope.

Quite often we got barked at and occasionally even chased by a dog. Nearly every cottage or house had a dog on a chain which hurled itself at each passing cyclist, barking and getting into a frenzy as it was yanked back by the chain which held it captive. A lot of these dogs seemed to live in old cars or vans – to which they were chained – and presumably they were guard-dogs whose frantic barkings were only valuable late at night. Not much of a life, though. Twenty square feet of dirt, a bowl of water and a burnt out car to call home.

The whole north-west coast seemed immensely self-sufficient. There was a lot of forestry work inland, and on the coast fishing and boat-building. Even the most modest fishing town or port had some kind of boat-building going on, both wooden and steel. And some of the boats were quite big, yet were being built at the water's edge with fairly elementary welding equipment and a small crane. Strangely, we never saw any fruit or vegetable markets in any of the towns or villages.

There was political graffiti everywhere, but almost all to do with regional struggles for autonomy and cultural identity. As often, political struggles were inextricably linguistic struggles too. In the Asturias and in Galicia, nearly all the road signs and municipal notices were defaced. The main grievance seemed to be over the continued use of a Romance language-based spelling against a Celtic-based spelling. Where the sign welcomed you to a regional 'Junta' (Council), the activists had replaced the J with X to read 'Xunta', and so on.

Quite a lot of the days began with a fairly long climb into the hills, on three occasions starting at sea-level and cycling for two hours in bottom gear to reach 2,000 feet by noon. Now this may sound like tortuous cycling, but it was often very gentle and almost un-noticeable some times. It all depended on the gradient. And then the rest of the day was spent slowly coming back to sea-level again. (A bit pointless some cynics might say; not really when the scenery around you, the fine weather, the smells of the wild herbs and clovers and trees, the kites and eagles circling overhead, the banal jokes and banter as people passed each other, all contributed to a very powerful feeling of separation and timelessness.) Ashbury used to put it rather differently: 'fucking character-building them hills, that's what it's all about'. And it is true, hill-climbing produces states of mind, self-questioning forms of introspection, mild and benign forms of solipsism, that are quite profound at times. Cheaper than analysis, and healthier than counselling, there is something quite therapeutic about a long, exhausting road climb.

It is surprising how easily and quickly the body recovers from occasional bouts of intense exertion – and the spirits also for that matter. You can find yourself nearing the top of a hill in the early afternoon sun, red-faced, sweating, heart banging about like a pigeon trapped inside a cake tin, and yet five minutes later free-wheeling down an open road, all senses fully recovered and ten minutes later swimming in a river and splashing about like a five year old, feeling as fresh and fit as if you'd just been born. If cycling allows you to gain access into your own mind and thoughts in unusual ways, it also enables you to develop a different relationship to your own body, expressed perhaps best in a question raised by the philosopher, William James: our bodies, are they *ours* or are they *us*? When you go cycling, it is your body you take on holiday, not your mind.

In the whole trip we only stayed in two cities, Santiago del Compostela in Spain and Oporto in Portugal where the trip ended. Santiago was very fine indeed, a medieval city still well preserved without too much fuss being made of it. A beautiful cathedral but with a rather over-the-top altar made of gold and looking more like a piece of fairground art rather than a serious religious artefact. Santiago is the fourth most important centre for pilgrimage in the world, because they claim to have the remains of St James the Apostle buried there, which were found in the ninth century. How anybody can seriously claim to recognise a body by a heap of bones 900 years old amazes me. Worshipping old bones seems more appropriate as a religion for dogs rather than human beings.

By the time we got to Portugal the temperatures were getting to be in the mid-80s by eleven in the morning and, what was worse, a lot of the roads were cobbled. This made cycling a nightmare, and so the last two days were the least enjoyable. Portugal was cheaper and much poorer. The tenements around the harbour in Oporto and the railway station were exactly how I imagined the Paris of *La Bohème* would have been. Tiny winding streets of very old dark tenements, washing everywhere, kids everywhere, rotting fruit in the gutters, and tiny noisy bars and cafes. Full of noise, of shouting and arguing and kids screaming and radios blaring. There were many beggars; kids asleep on the pavement; old people sitting outside the churches holding their hands out to every passer-by. But the churches, railway stations and houses in the older quarters were so spectacular, all of them tiled completely on the outside with blue and white ceramic tiles, with the most splendid murals and patterns.

After Oporto it was time to go home. Some people stayed for a few extra days; some returned by plane and some of us took the train back via Paris, a journey through Portugal, Spain and France which I had greatly looked forward to but which turned out to be pretty grim. The train was over-booked; the journey to Paris was 29 hours; and although we had a seat each in a crowded single compartment, the corridors were so full of luggage and sleeping people that it was impossible to move. The passengers were either small, dark-haired Portugese workers and their families returning to Paris where they lived and worked for most of the year, or tall, blond German and Danish students who had been all summer on the beaches of Portugal. And there was us. There was no buffet and although we'd all brought sandwiches, fruit and water, after 29 hours our mouths were like sandpaper. And even after that there was a rushed taxi-ride across Paris to catch the last night train to Dieppe and the ferry to Newhaven and another train home.

The lowest point of the holiday was on that last four hour ferry journey, having not slept for about 32 hours and been sitting cramped all that time. I was beyond exhaustion queuing to go on board. Struggling with my luggage I found a clear bit of floor space under the stairs on 'C' deck of this garish ferry, luckily out of hearing of the bar and the space invader machines. I unfurled my sleeping bag like a carpet salesman demonstrating a roll of Wilton and stretched out, with my head resting on one of the pannier bags. 'What are you trying to prove to yourself,' I thought. 'Downstairs in the bar are men much younger than you, probably earning less, who have parked their Ford Sierras on the car deck and are now enjoying their second gin and tonic. And yet you're here, unwashed and over-tired, stretched out on a dirty ferry deck floor, next to two young German hippies and an American motor-cyclist, as though you were still on the beatnik trail. What exactly is this all about?' But I fell asleep before I could give myself an answer.

6 London – Bordeaux – Barcelona October 1989

Suddenly summer is disappearing fast. The skies are overcast again; there is sporadic rain at night, and in the early morning; jackets are needed for cycling into town to pick up work. Up here in the attic room I call an office the wasps are drowsily trying to escape but no longer have the energy to climb up the glass of the opened sash windows and fly free into the clear air outside: they buzz desultorily, roll over on their stripy backs and die. All we can do now is wait for the photographs to come back from the chemists. Michaelmas daisies, one of the few flowers I've never learned to love – stringy, musty-smelling, over-tenacious, sepulchral – are everywhere, and every morning, stepping into the garden or along the front path one is trapped by webs of gossamer and spider trails. The long hot summer is over, and gone with it all the excuses for avoiding work; time to buckle down and embrace the Protestant ethic once again. I've even lost interest in watching television. How can we possibly adjust to the old routines again, yet how easily and unquestionably we do.

For Larraine and I it was a good summer (we bought a small boat on the River Lea), for Ben and Anna (for various reasons to do with jobs and holidays) disappointing and unsatisfactory. But everyone is now safe and sound again, and Ben and Anna off to the local polytechnic and sixth-form college respectively. *Dipper*, the boat, gave us days of relaxation and the pleasures of renovation, as well as some hours of apprehension bordering on mute horror as we negotiated our way through our first locks. It's such a small boat with enough room for two to sleep in, a cooker, stove, and handsome wooden fittings, but an engine that we have already discovered was probably taken from an old Foden lorry, together with a milk-float gearbox; the mechanics are held together by wire and string. It is ugly from the outside – Ben thinks it looks like a U-Boat – yet it has a peculiar charm of its own. There is no other boat like it on the Lea.

Springfield Marina has little or nothing in common with the conventional vision of marina life involving expensive yachts, gin and tonics, BMWs and beautiful young people wearing sunglasses on top of their heads. Springfield Marina, on the Hackney stretch of the River Lea, is like a an elephant's graveyard. Ancient cabin cruisers, dinghies, barge boats lay rested up in a fetid creek, propped up by old diesel cans and plastic milk crates, many having last been at sea before the war and likely not to see it again until the next. Their past glamour is not even a memory as the bare plywood shows through the once gleaming white hull, the metal fittings are rusted to oblivion, the paint has peeled everywhere, holes yawn in the deck, fibreglass decks have rotted away, and black bin liners flap in the wind where windows and gleaming portholes once used to be. There is dogshit everywhere. Springfield Marina is more like a wrecker's yard, yet here every evening and all weekend men – well mostly men – come with blow torches, electric drills, plastic filler and sandpaper, and spend hours on these wooden or fibreglass carcasses, filling, sanding, priming and painting, never getting anywhere, just idling the hours away in the open air, and dreaming of the sea. They drink tea, play cards, and no doubt moan about the wife or girlfriend as well. I would guess eight out of ten of all the boats moored at the Marina have not been actually on the river this year. They are ageing film stars, £25 scrap value masquerading as a £1 million dream: *Ocean Fiesta, Spindrift, Dad's Dream II, Potemkin, Easy Money, Spirit of Enfield, The Rebel.*

On the sluggish, weed-infested but occasionally dazzling river, gleaming narrow boats are now the thing, and very handsome they are with their folk-art watering-cans and coal buckets, and their window boxes full of geraniums and aubretia bordering the roof. There's clearly an appropriate style of dress ('English folk club' circa 1964) for the men and women among the narrow boat owners, who may even live on them rather than just use them at weekends or once a year. The men wear stout corduroy trousers or tight denim jeans, heavy leather ankle boots, waistcoats usually in black over collarless striped tunic shirts, finished off with a red neckscarf and a cloth cap pulled over the eyes. They roll their own cigarettes and usually have a dog tied with string to the cabin roof in front of them. The women are earth mother figures in jeans and men's shirts, often dandling young children in one arm while drinking tea or sketching with charcoals with their free hand.

These are now our peers and occasional companions – the fellowship of the river and patched up old boats seems disarmingly genuine and kind. Pottering about with a cup of tea and a paint brush down by the canal could become addictive. Five minutes by car from our house and you are away from the telephone, television, callers, teenagers, floppy disks, hoovers, listings magazines and diaries, and in a charmed world of willow trees, diesel oil, callused fingers, chemical toilets, roll your own cigarettes, tattoos, herons, swans, coots, moorhens and Canada Geese, and if you are lucky a tot of whiskey out of a dirty cup. Shall we gather by the river?

But this summer I also went cycling in France and Spain, cycling from Bordeaux to Barcelona, a journey of nearly five hundred miles. I went because the trip included crossing the Pyrenees, a mountain range with which for some reason I am obsessed. (Why? Because as the French *philosophes* had it, what was true on one side of the Pyrenees was not necessarily true on the other; because there are still bears living there; because Walter Benjamin committed suicide there; because I have seen them from the air and they are dazzling; because of the wild flowers; because of the way they sealed off a benighted Fascist regime from the rest of Europe for so many years, awkwardly, uncomfortably; because, finally, they divide the extraordinarily different and more exotic world of Spain and Portugal from the rest of rapidly homogenising Europe – but for how long?)

At the highest point we cycled to 6,500 feet, and camped near a Spanish village which at night produced the clearest sky and brightest stars I shall ever hope to see. Cold, indifferent, achingly splendid. But it wasn't a feat of endurance. Everybody who started, finished. Some cyclists were in their sixties, others in their teens; several were overweight and in not very good health. But long distance cycling is not necessarily a matter of stamina but of resilience. It's boring, at times, deeply tiring, hot, frustrating, only occasionally taxing on the lungs, legs and bum. But it requires no superhuman strength, abnormal muscle development, use of steroids, Union Jacks, travelling supporters, training from birth, right-wing political views, knowledge of quiz games, trips to South Africa, dual passports, or any of the other paraphernalia of 'serious' sports. You can smoke, drink, eat carp with a grape sauce, stay up late at night, go dancing, finish on calvados and cigars, and still do it – as long as you just love the symmetry of Reynolds 531 tubing, the grace and bounce of alloy wheels, and the sheer pleasure of a turning two pedals which translate every ounce of human endeavour into four times its value through a simple system of gears and wheels. In short, you either like bicycles and cycling (I do) or hate them. My own obsession, a matter of the last decade, has no rational explanation. I was never interested particularly as a teenager, yet somehow now I can't imagine life without two wheels.

Apart from a large Finsbury Park contingent, the only other strong geographical grouping was the crew who all came from Bath where the tour company is based. Perhaps it is the proximity to Glastonbury and the meeting point of all those ley lines, but people from the Bath area seem to inhabit a world of their own. The West Country seems detached in time and space from the rest of southern Britain. The same seven person crew provided the drivers for the four vehicles, the catering, the medical care, the folk-rock band; they were all multi-talented in that old hippie way in that they could mend bikes and cars, read Tarot cards, play Irish fiddle, talk at length on chaos theory or Jack Russell terriers, bluff their way into any 4-star restaurant and order 120 evening meals, drink half a bottle of brandy each and still be first up in the morning, opinionate at length on homeopathic medicine, and always be in between jobs. Everybody I've met from Bath has had elements of that rootless independence in them. What do they teach them in schools? I'm sure that when the national curriculum arrives, Bath schools will still insist on compulsory juggling and diesel engine maintenance lessons.

If the regular late night parties or four course restaurant meals in the evenings were the heady pleasures of the trip, the daytime pleasures were more of a miniaturist nature. Getting up, packing up tents, shaving and chewing muesli were mostly done in a state of lethargy and mild apprehension of the day's cycling to come. There were only two kinds of day: a short distance up a very steep mountain or a long ride up a gentle set of foothills. We were blessed with perfect weather. As any cyclist will tell you, the first ten miles of the day are the worst; here any aches and pains, discomfitures, old muscle problems, creaking joints, rapidly assert their own identity and you wonder if you will ever finish the day's ride. After ten miles a rhythm is established, all the aches and pains disappear, and in the right circumstances, you begin to achieve a state of otherness, nirvana, or mindless boredom, whichever particular metaphysics one subscribes too.

The great thing about large amounts of exhausting physical exercise is that it nullifies all other physical and mental concerns. There are no agonies of indecision in the morning as to what has to be done and in what order – there is only one choice: you lift your leg over the saddle, put your feet in the toe-clips, and start cycling. At the end of the day your brain is so numbed by tiredness that you enter a pleasant state of mental and intellectual vacuity. Like an automaton, you dismount, find your bags and tent, put up the tent, have a shower and then lay out on the grass for an hour staring into the sun.

So what was cycling through the Pyrenees actually like? Well the two days on the flat in south-west France were idyllic. Gentle hills, winding country roads, small villages and a great variety of farming, forestry, landscapes and people. It still felt very religious, as the many roadside shrines to the Virgin Mary were well kept with fresh flowers and pristine paintwork. Only subsequently did I realise how much I prefer inhabited landscapes to uninhabited ones, for the further into the Pyrenees we went the less people, houses or any sign of human cultivation we saw, and the bleaker it became. The second night we camped in the medieval town of Armagnac, found the best bar of the whole trip, friendly, ridiculously cheap, with an outside garden overhung with vines, with a dark interior of old woodwork and ancient prints and photographs of football and cycling teams. The field we camped in was just one thick carpet of wild mint, which, crushed by the tents and people's constant footsteps, gave off such a sickly smell that one slept as if drugged.

Further into the French Pyrenees we came into the smarter winter ski resorts such as Luchon, but since it is a principle of these bike tours that main roads are never used – even where the main roads are the only roads – we found ourselves cycling along goat tracks and roads of scree over the tops of mountains rather than through the valleys from town to town. Some of these wild mountain roads were fabulous as you cycled clear of the gulches, rivers and forests, above the tree-line and into the hot, clear air of cropped pastures and dizzying heights. It was not unusual to be cycling along a mountain road looking down into the valley on the tiny Cessna aircraft used for local air traffic flying below, looking down on the hang-gliders, and on to the world beneath settled comfortably on the valley floor like a model railway set on the front room carpet. For a number of days we climbed some 2,000 feet in the morning only to drop down 1,500 feet again in the afternoon to the next village and campsite. But oh the exhilaration of some of those views and spectacles – valleys folding into each other like bolts of cloth unravelled, layers of mountains standing in serried rows further and further into the distance like a pop-up book picture, sunlight and shadows moving across the valleys like a stain spreading in water. It all felt so expansive, so utopian. And what was best was the silence. And the wind ruffling the gorse bushes, the occasional long grasses, the sheep's fleece caught in the scrub.

But the increasing remoteness of the landscape meant that on some days there simply were no bars, hamlets or villages to be cycled through from the start of the ride until the end. A single road across a mountain or through a long gorge could be cycled along for hours without seeing a single car or lorry. This made one feel better about being able to cycle in the middle or, when negotiating the frequent hairpin bends, on the wrong side of the road, as often one found oneself riding within three or four feet of a sheer drop of some hundreds of feet into rock-strewn river or forested gorge. It sounds worse than it felt at the time; just a case of keeping awake, that's all. The compensations for this isolation – which others enthused about more than I did – were that the occasional stop for a piss, a drink of water, a bar of chocolate or a handful of prunes, involved finding a secluded resting place by a stream or in a glade, in which you quickly realised just how profuse and fecund the natural flora and fauna really were. In less than five minutes one night see at least six different kinds of grasshopper, dozens of different moths and butterflies, several kinds of lizards, dragonflies and lots of other bugs and divers creepy-crawlies. The grass was alive with insects, pulsating with movement. Quite extraordinary. The only disappointing thing was the lack of variety of birds – hardly any at all except for the occasional large bird of prey, a buzzard or a kite, a few magpies and sparrows. We saw several fields full of crocuses – in the autumn!

The ride into Barcelona was the low point of the holiday – suburbs, motorways, industrial estates, dust and noise everywhere, and later very fast traffic and impatient drivers. But the city centre lived up to every expectation I had of it and had been told about; it teems with life night and day; it is a city which the people (as 'the people') still live in and territorially control the centre, which is full of tiny streets and alleys teeming with tenements, bars, small shops and street life. We only had one day in the city before the 28 hour train/boat/train journey back to Victoria.

I was pleased to realise on this trip that I am now regarded by others as a competent long distance cyclist. Whereas in earlier trips I had often been at the back, distinctly ruffled and frazzled by the end of a day's ride, on this trip within an hour of finishing and endless cups of tea and a shower, I felt fully revived and ready for anything. It is difficult really to explain the hold that cycling eventually has over people. In the winter months, just to look at my touring bike hanging upside down in the shed brings a profound sense of well-being, and anticipation of pleasures and freedoms still to come. It is like a lifeline and a passport to another world.

7 London – Sigoules, France September 1991

Anarchy in the UK? When Larraine and I arrived back in London last week, after two weeks in France, the political world had simply and astonishingly changed. The coup and counter-coup in Moscow had seemed to deal the final blow to the global ideal of world communism, and the left everywhere seemed to be reeling. Communism in practice, it was concluded, almost invariably produced authoritarianism, intellectual and political censorship, massive moral corruption and economic stagnation – all the things I had once understood it was destined to replace. Did our dream of a self-governing, internationalist, world-wide republic of citizens and equals really not get beyond the rhetoric of the Friday night meeting or the composite resolution? Was socialism in the end just fine words mouthed by self-deluding and self-aggrandising intellectuals left out in the cold?

I still think that the ideal of communist internationalism did bring long term effects for the good in some ways, enabling millions to live lives with a degree of self-respect and a sense of their own agency. If it failed as a system of large scale government, then as a world-wide oppositional ethic and organising principle of most anti-colonial struggles it is going to be difficult to better. That is why its defeat is so sobering and difficult to acknowledge. But anarchy next? I ask this because the day after we got back and were feeling low about being surrounded once again by dirty streets and a general sense of anomie in the north London air, we went over to Hackney Downs where an Anti-Fascist Action pop concert was being organised, to do our duty as civic elders. The weather was stupendously hot for September, a baking Sunday afternoon, and the crowds were out in force – the biggest political event in Hackney I've seen for years. But Larraine and I hardly recognised anybody. The left we knew had disappeared, or was still on holiday, and in its place were thousands of tattooed, earringed, shaven-headed or dread-locked punks and squatters, with dogs on bits of string, cider bottles in their hands, clutching plastic bags with bits of bread in them and looking like a lost army from the Hundred Years War. This, we realised, was the new political movement.

Hackney has had squatters for years, but I hadn't realised just how large this subculture had become. It now completely dwarfs all others. This ragged army have cut their political teeth in the anti-Poll Tax riots and fighting the Council bailiffs, and they regard the conventional left with disdain and even venom. Whether this is a purely East London phenomenon I don't know, but it's pretty sobering.

Astonishingly there were no papersellers to be seen. Radical organisations had been allowed an area of the field to set up their stalls, and an air of confusion and disarray hung over the various communist or trotskyist stalls, with their thinner than usual papers and manifestos only half-heartedly calling for workers' councils in post-coup Soviet Union, or arming the people to resist the state. Nobody was looking, let alone buying – with two exceptions. The Class War stall seemed pretty busy, but the real action was at the anarchist stall where anarchist and situationist literature seemed to be selling as fast as Big Macs in the Nevsky Prospekt.

I fear that the vacuum left by the collapse of communism and the historic British socialist ideal (which I am sure will be recovered in time, possibly quite quickly) is going to be filled in the immediate future with the sporadic riot, subcultural retreat, and general political alienation. Do I sound old-fashioned? The reason I worry, or feel sad, is not because the occasional dust-up with the Old Bill amounts to very much, but that so many young people feel totally betrayed by the political process – by the svelte plump men in suits in the mainstream political parties or the self-righteous, self-opinionated cadres of the organised left groups. And this negativism doesn't just take the form of the occasional bottle-throwing; it's become very much more personalised and internalised in the form of a self-hatred and sense of hopelessness, most strongly marked by the heavy tattooing and body-piercing now the rule rather than the exception among the crowd we saw there, both women and men.

This was not the occasional arm or shoulder tattoo but was often covering large parts of the upper body and face, further ornamented by large numbers of rings and studs stuck into ears, noses, lips, nipples, and cheeks. In short, this was serious self-mutilation, and it disturbed me. Discussing it with Dave the other night, when we met for a drink in the local pub, his criticisms of this substantial local culture were that its members had elevated a sense of transience to a new level. Other individuals and cultures settling in Hackney in the fairly recent past – West Indians, Asians, the middle-class intelligentsia, yuppies – had made a point of trying to make connections and if necessary re-define a new sense of locality around their own arrival and presence, often quite positively. These young people simply don't want to make any connections. Even eye contact is impossible, said Dave, confirming my own experiences. One nods a friendly tentative kind of acknowledgement to many of the squatters in our street – there are lots of them – and they look right through you.

So in times of difficulty, take the long view. Say one million years. On holiday I read pre-history studies voraciously, starting with Stephen Jay Gould's *Wonderful Life*, and finishing with one of Ben's student texts, a large compendium of essays by and on Darwin and his contemporaries. In between I read, shamefacedly I admit, for the first time, Gilbert White's *Selbourne*, the founding text of English naturalist observation, and, I realise, the very same activating spirit at work to record and register as lies behind these letters. And also at long last Keith Thomas' massive tome on *Religion and the Decline of Magic*. Nothing contemporary at all, and yet somehow pervasive to our times or to my own thoughts and concerns. Gould's book is a re-interpretation of fossil discoveries made in Canada at the beginning of this century which confound the thesis of continual evolution upwards, and instead, suggests contingency, randomness, accident, uneven development and even regression. In short there were some brainier molluscs and bivalves around one million years ago which could have developed into something more interesting than homo sapiens except that their small lives got cut short by various ice-age catastrophes. Gould, more importantly, is a witty and elegant writer, with a facility for communicating complex ideas with a literary style that one would die for.

The Keith Thomas book interested me because I'm still slowly trying to come to terms with the major structures of thought and feeling which have dominated European popular consciousness in the past few hundred years, and clearly the mythical, magical and superstitious have represented a long-standing way of understanding and trying to influence the world. Thomas' book shows how the church at the time of the Reformation both incorporated the old pagan rituals and practices, and slowly rationalised them, though the tensions between catholic ritual and protestant austerity and scepticism remains a powerful cultural bi-polarity to this day. Of course there's a personal angle. My grandmother, a formidable figure in Mile End culture at the turn of the century, remained wholly governed by superstition to the end of her life, traces of which are still to be found in my mother's attitude to the contingencies of daily life.

I only knew my grandmother at two addresses, two small cottages in Chelmsford, where she and my grandad had moved during the war, because he worked for Taylor Walker's brewery which re-located there from Stepney after the Blitz. Before the war they had been small time East London swells, he a street bookmaker and *flâneur*, with white silk scarf, and a smoking habit of 80 cigarettes a day, and she a popular pub pianist and local money-lender. She was hard and shrewd, he benign and loveable. In their small clapboard cottage, there were always dead rabbits hanging up in the outside larder, the racing pages open on the table, and their daily life was organised to fit in with the 3.30 at Kemptown or the 4.15 from Chepstow.

I stayed there sometimes during school holidays. I could write about it for hours, but I won't. Except to recall that for my grandmother particularly, life was synonymous with fate, with pre-determination, with chance; her world-view was a *mélange* of astrological pre-destination together with spilt salt and broken mirror contingency. Every afternoon a succession of women sat in the kitchen to chat and have their tea-leaves read. She was considered a gifted interpreter of tea-leaves. She shuddered and reached for something to hold on to if you were out shopping with her and a black cat crossed your path; may blossom wasn't allowed into the house, shoes not allowed to be put on a table, mirrors were turned to the wall and the cutlery covered up during a thunderstorm. Horoscopes were read first thing in the morning and ruminated upon, Old Moore's Almanac consulted for supporting or countervailing prognostication, lucky brooches and rabbit's feet clips were pinned to her 'going out' coat, charm bracelets and crucifixes worn around her arms and neck. She thanked God in mumbled tones at least 20 times a day, and for additional protection stroked her rabbit's foot brooch. In brief, she incarnated that long-standing overlap between magical and Christian belief which allegedly was resolved in the seventeenth century. However at her death in the late 1970s, a generation after the advent of the welfare state, she still embodied a complex system of quasi-magical, pagan and monotheistic beliefs that were no different from someone living 400 years ago.

In contrast, whereas Nan Elvin picked her horses with closed eyes and a pin, Grandad Elvin studied 'form' with the intellectual sophistication of a quantum physicist. A believer in multiple causation, synergy and Heisenberg's 'Uncertainty Principle', for every race he calculated the past successes of the horse, the particular qualities of the horse's sire and dam, the weight of the jockey and the jockey's personality, the length of the course and the going conditions, wind direction, and weighed them against the likely odds, a proletarian form of cost-benefit analysis. He lost a lot of money.

Talk of books read, and secondary digressions into childhood reminiscences, is by way of alluding to the fact that Larraine and I have been travelling again. We hired a cheap cottage in a small village near Bergerac in the Dordogne (we subsequently discovered why it was so cheap), and spent most of the days reading, taking photographs or bird-watching, and in the late afternoons went swimming in a nearby lake. In the evenings we alternated cooking in or eating out in nearby hotels and restaurants, always asking for the *menu de jour* or *menu prix fixe*, and it was almost as cheap as staying at home. But it was certainly different. I think like many people of our generation who were the first in their families to go abroad (except to war), France and the other Mediterranean countries will always be associated with an unshackling, a sense of freedom. A break from austerity mixed with images from the posters we hung on our first bed-sit rooms – scenes of white-washed rooms overlooking a brilliant blue sea, with geraniums or cornflowers, by painters such as Matisse or Dubuffet. Primary colours and shapes rather than *Picture Post* photo-realism or washed out English water-colours. A new sensibility in fact, that overwhelmed me when Larraine and I first went together to Yugoslavia, after we got married in 1965, and opened the shutters in a tiny room in Dubrovnik on to the dazzling sea below. I think then we realised that we would lead very different lives from those of our parents.

In France, the weather was stupendously hot. Days of clear skies and hot suns followed each other like guests at a wedding. The house was a tiny terrace house in a small square, in the centre of which sat a crumbling church, whose loud bells rang twice every hour, a minute to the hour and a minute after, starting at 6 am and finishing at 10 pm. The loudness and suddenness of the bells rocked the square, and woke us each morning with a sudden shock as if startled by a pistol shot.

The back half of the house had its roof open to the sky and at some time in the past had been burnt out. The ramshackle terrace to which it belonged was built with walls at least 18 inches thick, clearly fortified, with crude giant timber joists running east to west, and floorboards nailed directly on to them, with no panelling or false ceilings underneath. The woodworking was crude, and it felt like living in a just slightly renovated castle tower. All the beams were totally rotten, some eaten away to a third of their original thickness, and although they had been treated, this was the cause of yet another problem: the little house stank of timber preservative and gave us headaches and nightmares, even with all the windows and doors open at night. Well at least that was one possible explanation. Every footstep creaked, was amplified and reverberated through the shell of the house. If this was a ship, you would not have sailed across the bathtub in it. One climbed the home made stairs with hands holding on to every available fixture. But it was deeply cool in the day, and so we read enormously and enjoyably every morning after doing the shopping. But at night the house came into its own, a ghostly, creaking, echoing medieval well.

Plato's philosophy – and subsequent traditions of philosophical idealism – was based on the idea that beyond our knowing were the ideal forms of everything – tables, chairs, concepts of beauty and truth: according to Platonism we live in a cave facing the inner wall and only see the shadows thrown upon the wall by the bright light outside. This life is just a shadow of a more authentic, pristine world beyond. If there was an ideal, typical, quintessential and therefore Platonic French village, then Sigoules, where we stayed, was it. Medieval, perched on a slight hill, housing about four hundred people in the village with another six hundred in new houses on the periphery, it contained a hotel, a bar, a post office, a bank, three hairdressers, a newsagent, a bakery, a butcher's, a delicatessen, three mini-markets, a florist, a police-station and a church. The people seemed used to visitors and were mostly friendly and *charmant.* While we were there a circus came to the village for just one night. It was a pitiful affair and we couldn't convince ourselves to go. The tent went up in the afternoon, the two flea-bitten mangy llamas pegged to the nearby grass verge, the monkey-cage put out in the sun, and the clowns' uniforms pegged out to dry. A loudspeaker van toured the village for just one afternoon, and by 9.30 the next morning they had disappeared without a trace.

For us the most engaging feature was the dining room of the *Hôtel du Centre* – the Central Hotel. Nobody ever stayed there as far as we knew. The dining-room was a ballroom-sized space, filled with tables and chairs, and invariably empty. Occasionally men played cards at one of the tables, escaping from the juke-box in the adjoining bar; the local policeman stopped by for a sandwich. Yet it had a beauty all of its own: large French windows opened out on to the square and the balmy evening air. Bereft of almost any adornment apart from the lino-covered tables, it also contained astonishingly, a giant elaborate glass bookcase in the Louis Quinze style, with a complete *Encyclopaedia Britannica,* a complete *Flora and Fauna of France,* and a number of other leather-bound books. There was also a large desk by the kitchen at which the woman manager took your order, so high she disappeared behind it. But she was delightfully friendly, the food was very simple, very cheap and very good, and so we sat in there on a number of nights by the open windows, intoxicated by the wine and the sticky night air, the echoing sounds of the village – voices, car doors slamming, snatches of TV game shows, motor bikes, barking dogs – cocooned in a sense of well-being and suspension in time and space.

The surrounding landscape was also very lovely, comprised as it was mostly of cornfields, fields of sunflowers, vineyards, meadowland and the occasional broad-leaf copse or wood. Buzzards and red kites were as common as magpies in England. At first I was astonished to see the first of these great birds fly low across the road, but we became blasé about them. The kites often perched on corn stooks and could be seen through the binoculars in close detail, often at a distance of no more than 30 yards. I also saw a golden oriole in close up, when it flew into my sights and settled while I was looking at two other birds perched in a dead tree. The whole landscape is criss-crossed with long straight roman roads, totally empty of traffic, only connecting tiny villages and hamlets, often at many miles distance from each other.

In the middle of our fortnight we drove over to see some friends who were staying about 60 miles away and stayed overnight. The house they were in was deep in the middle of a very old forest, along a dirt track through woodland and finally into a clearing. It was very dark and spooky at night. Only 400 yards away, on one side of a valley, stood an eleventh century castle, built upon rocks containing hundreds of caves that had been lived in by early human groups of hunters and gatherers. That dark, damp, narrow winding valley was palpably haunted. In these caves had been found the most marvellous early sculptures and rock carvings, dating back to about 15,000 BC. The next day we visited Lascaux.

Geoff and Helen were staying in the valley of Les Eyzies, perhaps the most famous of all the early human settlements which left behind evidence of its life and culture. The story of the discovery of Lascaux is well known. Four boys and a dog playing in the woods in 1940 came across a hole in the ground, leading to a cave in which there were paintings of the most astonishing richness and detail. The caves were opened to the public after the war but closed in 1963 because of the damage done by the presence of so many visitors. A reconstruction has been built beneath the ground 200 yards way from the original, and these were the caves we saw, every detail of the size and shape of the caves reconstructed to the nearest millimetre, with the paintings copied using the same materials and methods as the originals, 15,000 years before them. It couldn't have been more stunning and overwhelming even if they had been the originals. We were both greatly entranced by these great, colourful, expressive paintings of animals, filling every inch of the tiny, narrow caves.

Several years ago I had seen the Giotto frescoes in Tuscany, and subsequently began lecturing people, even hectoring them, on the discovery of perspective, and the development of humanism in medieval art. The Lascaux paintings, from a culture allegedly primitive, demonstrated a clear sense of perspective, and an expressivity and emotional engagement with colour and form that simply didn't reappear again, as far as I can understand, until the late nineteenth and early twentieth century. These giant bison heads, and horses' faces writhed and breathed fire, their bodies strained every sinew, they demonstrated the most expressive energy and movement. Yet the only illustration of a human being found in these caves was of a crude stick man, raising one of the first of many still unsolved questions surrounding the meaning and nature of these great works of art.

Various theories have been advanced and subsequently rejected. The range of animals depicted neither tallies with the animals they ate nor the animals they feared or worshipped. Why some and not others? The caves they chose to decorate were pretty small and inaccessible – they could not have been used as religious meeting places or even shrines because of their awkward size and shape. And why, given that they could paint animals so brilliantly, could they not draw or paint a human figure other than in the form of the crudest stick man? Lastly, what were the strange markings that were laid over every painting, as if a signature, which were also found on cave paintings in Spain hundreds of miles away and possibly several thousands of years later? I think it was the mystery about these great splashes of colour and form, the intensity of the lines which represented the leaping animals, that entranced us. One felt a great affinity and respect for the people who did these paintings, a closeness in fact. These astonishing cave paintings 'spoke' to me in a way that no gallery paintings ever have done.

If our days were wonderful, the nights were less so. For some reason, neither of us could sleep at all well, and such sleep we had was riven by endless dreams and nightmares. I think in that fortnight every person I have ever known, good or bad, alive or now dead, visited me in that upstairs creaking room, in some phantasmagoric or bizarre scenario. Two German friends came to stay for a few days and they too had terrible dreams every night. Was it the heat, the creaking rooms, or possibly the chemicals used to preserve what remained of the wood?

But back to the discussion of Thomas' book on seventeenth century religion and magic. I remember reading somewhere that Leslie Stephen, Virginia Woolf's father, thought that the Protestant Reformation was the unwitting precursor of rationalism and, consequently, the Enlightenment. One connection which fascinates me between the last days of magic and the first days of logic is the belief in the divine efficacy of drawing lots. Cromwell drew lots to decide which regiments to send to Ireland, believing that God would probably arrange the straws. Many eminent institutions, including the Church, came to decisions by the drawing of lots. Eager, as always, to perceive some great hidden plan or scheme behind things, an interest was developed in the laws of probability, in statistical recurrence as a basis for making laws or advocating reform. At the time of the French Revolution there was much debate about acceptable percentages of error in sending innocent or guilty people to the guillotine, which took the form of deciding the size of juries and whether simply majority verdicts should suffice, rather than unanimous verdicts or near-unanimous ones. The Belgian Astronomer- Royal, Adolphe Quetelet, devised a calculation based on statistical evidence to produce a cast-iron formula for predicting when the lilacs would bloom in the Brussels parks.

But then probability seemed to be – and in some ways still does – in complete opposition to the notion of free will. For example – and as you will realise, I am still trying to get to grips with statistical probability myself – every act of suicide is an act of individual volition, every car crash a unique combination of arbitrary and fortuitous events, yet every year in Britain almost exactly the same number of people will kill themselves or die in a motor accident. How does a set of unpredictable occurrences reach a critical mass of inevitability? When I was at school maths was unproblematically precise, but today they do study probability theory, which I think I would like to do. Obsessed as I am by each new book I read, I asked Ben if he had studied probability at school. 'Probably,' he said.

Gilbert White's *The Natural History of Selbourne* is the fourth most published book in the English language, and as I said earlier, I'm embarrassed that I've only just got round to reading it. For it is a seminal kind of writing within the English literary tradition. Selbourne is a real village in Hampshire, and White lived and died there in the eighteenth century. He was the vicar and died in a house 100 yards from where he was born. The book consists entirely of letters he wrote to a friend describing the weather, topography, flora and fauna of his small village. That's all. Yet it confirms that sense of the importance of detail which suggests that all the great discoveries are made at home. White identified many new plants and insects, reflected deeply on evolution, natural diversity, generic modification or innovation, yet rarely wandered far from his front door. The world in a grain of sand, or at most five acres. I'm very sympathetic to that point of view.

The reason that this letter has proceeded so quickly, is that at present there is hardly any work around at all. August and September are usually quiet but this is sepulchral. I'm driven to finishing off bits and pieces of work for which I can claim money from somewhere, things I've usually left to 'the last'. Now 'the last' has arrived. No doubt an election will clear the air, one way or another. Communism is dead, work is drying up, someone let the air out my tyres yesterday in central London. Why do I feel so resolutely cheerful?

8 London – East Berlin March 1985 and March 1989

I *March 1985*

It was the train journey on the North East Europe Express, which we caught at the Hook of Holland, that gave us our first impression and feeling of being involved in an inter-war spy film with crowded carriages filled with incongruous Europeans being shunted off in all directions through the night. Every carriage on the train went somewhere different, and was marked accordingly. Many of the carriages came from different national rolling stock – from Denmark, Poland, Russia, Hungary, East Germany – and about every hour during the night the train stopped and carriages were coupled and uncoupled and sent flying off down other historical tracks, whilst our little world of course seemed to be the only true and proper journey, the one that the train had always been meant for.

We – myself and two other literature enthusiasts – were wedged into a compartment for six, with six people in it and at least fifteen suitcases. One person in our compartment was an elderly Polish woman with an unbelievably sad and gentle face, who was returning back across the Iron Curtain to Poland after visiting her Dutch married daughter. She had about twelve different bags with her, and her leave-taking at the station was the most distressing and poignant I have ever seen. She was quite old and she pressed her face to the window, as her daughter did on the other side of the glass, and they kept kissing their hands and pressing them against the glass so that they were kind of joined in prayer. And as the train finally pulled out, the despair of the woman at leaving her daughter again to travel all the way across Europe back to a tormented country was felt by everyone in our carriage. She talked to herself and wept. Then she turned around to us all and gave us the most wonderful smile. And she smiled at us for all of the rest of the journey. At every possible occasion she touched us as if we were all her children. She squeezed our arms, and finally went to sleep massaging the leg of a young Dutch woman who sat opposite her and had put her feet up.

Apart from the three of us, there was the Polish woman, the young Dutch woman with her Walkman which just produced the drum beats for everybody else, and an olive-complexioned woman whom we quickly discovered was a woman lawyer from Nicaragua doing a speaking tour of Europe to raise support for the Sandinistas. So we bought coffees all round, the Dutch girl passed round some (disgusting) liquorice sticks, the Nicaraguan woman passed round some biscuits, and we all got quite cosy and familiar, although not one person could understand one word of what anyone else said – except the English contingent. And all the time the Polish woman looked at us all and smiled. And that is how we travelled through the night until dawn brought us to the border and the beginning of a different social and cultural trajectory in post-war European history: a certain kind of visible austerity, formality, over-militarisation of daily life, weak tea, queues, and a strong sense of deference towards all people in uniform that seemed to me from the start just impossible. It is not nice to see people nervous when there's a uniform about.

We were here at the invitation of Humboldt University to present papers at a conference on English Working-Class Literature, which is a subject taken immensely more seriously here than it is in Britain itself. In the teleology of international proletarian culture, English literature and English writers (notably Irish, Welsh and Scots writers in fact) are regarded as having set standards and achievements that others must follow. And it is true, the body of significant fiction writing by coal miners and ex-miners alone in Britain between the wars is an impressive achievement, not that many would know this from the critical attention this work has received in its own country of origin. But I'm here as much to try to understand this wholly different kind of social system as I am to give a lecture on the work of three Liverpool-Irish seaman writers: George Garrett, James Hanley and Jim Phelan.

The conference is held in a trade union rest home and summer camp about 75 miles outside Berlin, near the Polish border. I am writing this in a free hour after dinner on a borrowed typewriter in my dormitory room. Borrowing a typewriter was difficult enough in itself, but borrowing paper was almost impossible. It is worth pursuing a short digression about paper in the GDR. In the West a new virtue has evolved, involving turning used and unwanted paper into bricks. Here, it seems, the opposite applies: bricks are turned into paper. The typing paper, writing paper, newspapers and even toilet paper all seem to have been shaved off of old rough bricks – grey and harsh and lumpy. Last night I wiped my face on a paper towel that felt it had been shaved off an old English Fletton. The paper shortage also means that books are sold out the day they are published, as the print runs are so small.

The rain is beating on the window. Twenty feet away the black waters of the lake are beating away at the banks and smashing against the trees at the water's edge. I've just come back from a walk round the lake, getting back just as the wind was picking up and both the sky and the water turned an ominous black. Here they have terrifying hooded crows, grey bodies with black heads and wing tips. They give me the creeps. Before that we were entertained, after dinner, by five fresh-faced young Berliners who belong to a folk group called The Larkins – named not after H.E. Bates' ebullient family but after Dublin trade union hero Jim Larkin – who sing songs about Nicaragua, Northern Ireland, international proletarian solidarity and German folk songs about bears in the snow, with an innocence that it is terribly emotional and affecting, because to our ears it is just too naive. Like singing 'We Shall Overcome' when you have just been overcome. In your bones you know that this political system and culture is heading inexorably towards defeat. The Larkins were managed and coached by a Scots émigré who lives in the GDR and teaches at the university and is, not surprisingly, a dedicated communist. He lives and operates within an over-arching system of belief in the irreversible progress of scientific history, day one of which was 17 October, 1917 in Russia. Everything is moving inevitably towards a given end. On the other hand, he is amazingly well read, a fine folk-singer, a good poet, an optimist, a reader and critic with a wide understanding of world literature, a much travelled man, and very good company too.

The conference is dreadfully formal and formulaic. This afternoon we listened to no less than eight papers, all read word by word from prepared texts, with no asides, off the cuff remarks or explications, or indeed any kind of personal exegesis at all. For the most part literature has been weighted down and submerged in theory and set phrases and formulations – bourgeois subjectivism, principles of marxism-leninism, concrete reality, social Darwinism, and so on – yet all the contributors, when not standing on the platform, are among the nicest people you could ever wish to meet. In this austere but not unfriendly country, the vocabulary of scientific socialism is simply part of the air that people breathe. Unselfconsciously too. One impressive thing is that people will genuinely argue all the time about everything and I learnt that all academic dissertations have to be presented publicly and defended against whoever turns up to take issue with the thesis.

The diet at the conference centre is completely meat-centred – it is all blood puddings, brawn, various kinds of salami, and the bones of God knows what animal in the soup. There's a lot of fat, gristle and skin. All the fruit and vegetables are tinned. Everything about the way of life reminds me of my own childhood years – utility furniture, dull shops, tinned food, shop items being wrapped in poor quality sugar paper. In the GDR, the joke goes, a plastic carrier bag is a design accessory. Ninety per cent of the cars here are tiny things called Trabants which seem to have sewing-machine engines in them. Nothing more than 400 cc I'm sure. They go all right, but with a high-pitched whine, and the crashing of gears without synchro-mesh. Our two hosts in Berlin drive like there's no tomorrow, just missing great steel trams by inches, sliding all over the place on wet cobbles and greasy tram lines, crashing from one pot-hole to the next.

From one pot-hole to the next – that's the road history takes I believe. When we arrived in Berlin it was winter, when we left it was summer. Well into the 70s and people in shorts and T-shirts. Just like that! Even they were astonished. On our last day back in Berlin we walked around and visited museums and things and sat in bars in the Unter den Linden drinking beers and coffee on tables outside, under umbrellas. Yet Andy reminded us that the opening sentence in Isherwood's *Goodbye to Berlin* is, 'It was spring in the Unter den Linden, and the Nazis were in power.' The anti-fascist struggle is ubiquitous here – monuments, posters, an eternal flame over two unknown soldiers in a giant Doric-columned sarcophagus.

Our three guides on our last full day in Berlin were young women who had been at the conference, literature post-graduates, two of whom were ex-gymnasts with rather serious faces which occasionally broke into girlish laughter. They were all in their mid-twenties and were all Party members. They had the poise and affecting innocence of three sixth-formers showing visitors around their school on open day. We went to the cemetery where Brecht, Hans Eisler, Helen Weigel and Hegel were buried. 'This is Brecht's grave. Of course he had some criticisms of the party but he also understood the need for party unity and final acceptance of the programme of the SED.' So we walked, ate ice-cream, told bad jokes, looked at the wall, took photographs of each other and exchanged addresses.

All the people we met were kind and hospitable. Nothing was too much or too inconvenient. We slept in three different people's flats and they fed us, took us out to restaurants, made lovely breakfasts for us and wanted to talk well into small hours about the necessity for the GDR 'road' or 'programme'. They believed that 'actually existing socialism' had been deeply misunderstood and travestied in the western press and though they acknowledged many problems, they were all convinced of the rightness of their way of building socialism. At night the streets were quiet, with no sign of the police, and a great deal of self-policing as it were. The underground trains and the buses were clean and tidy all day long, people were reserved but friendly, most certainly a woman could walk through the city and subways at one in the morning without a worry. It had that feeling of tremendous bourgeois respectability which is of course what the leading struggle of the working-class project is all about. All prices were fixed and printed directly on to items for sale, whether beer bottles or butter wrappers. Inflation was illegal under the constitution! But every record shop I visited had the same 28 records for sale, whether people wanted them or not. This year jazz meant two Louis Armstrong, one Art Pepper, one Ben Webster and two Polish jazz LPs. That was all. Take it or leave it. Production and distribution of cultural goods particularly seemed totally arbitrary and quite unmatched to any notion of what people might actually want. Hence the black market.

And there's also a problem, which many people admitted, of the absence of any kind of public service ideal in face to face dealings in shops and institutions. Bank clerks were often downright rude, shop-workers indifferent; restaurant waiters pretended there were no free tables when the restaurant was three-quarters empty. Everybody deferred instantly to any official in uniform, clearly out of fear. This was mostly at the border, and with the customs, but generally people were very disciplined, externally and internally. Many of the friends we made said this was a Prussian legacy that had been absorbed into the East German socialist project.

And what of my fellow-travellers ? Well Paul was 32, from Bolton, had been a railway worker for a number of years and even a full-time Communist Party organiser for a while too: one of the nicest people I've met in years. Now works as a community worker and WEA tutor, has joined the Labour Party and has published a lot of material on Lancashire socialism and working-class dialect poetry. There was something of the earnest schoolboy about him, a fanatical train-spotter who nearly got us shot on several occasions as he jumped into the paths of oncoming Soviet trains or GDR steam trains to get pictures of legendary 1937 steam engines from the Great Proletarian Engine Works in Vladivostock or other great works of railway heavy engineering or rolling stock. At Friedrichstrasse station waiting for the train to leave the GDR (while it was searched twice by armed guards, and while sniffer dogs were let loose under the engine and carriages) he innocently walked about eighty yards over the forbidden white line at the end of the platform to get a picture of the engine.

Andy is, I think, 28 and another earnest Party member who knows more about English literature in the 1930s and 1940s than anybody else I've ever met. He has a fund of stories about Auden, Isherwood, and forgotten working-class writers who ended up living in the Soviet Union, and was able to provide further details about every writer or book mentioned throughout the whole conference, including what the provisional titles for their first novels had been, what they had said to Dimitroff when they bumped into him on Platform No 8 at the Gare de Lyon on their way to the 1934 Soviet Writers Congress and so on.

It was the very best kind of experience: to travel with friends to another country where one would be both a guest and yet also a contributor. To go with a purpose. A lot of the new architecture is monolithic, endless apartment buildings in stone with semi-ornate façades lining great wide roads which run straight for miles, four lanes each way with wide pavements and trees down the sides. Designed for easy access by tank, like Paris was rebuilt by Haussman with wide avenues for the cavalry after the 1870

Commune. The old buildings are heavily gothic and ornate, still pebble-dashed with bullet and mortar marks. Yet the space did have a sense of its own. The new society is still possible there with a lot more trees and a wider range of consumer goods – particularly records and books. The week will stay with me for ever. I was very happy there all the time. That is why I wanted to write this letter. To fix the memories in words like a chemical fixes the image of a photograph. Otherwise memories have a habit of contracting and becoming just diffuse general feelings over time.

I'm very unsure about those wide avenues. They're nice to walk down in the warm evening air, under the trees, yet the perspective forward and when you look behind always seems to remain the same, *as if you will never actually reach the place you want to get to.* Karl Marx Allee must be about three miles long and it is one long straight avenue, nearly a quarter of a mile wide. It's a bit creepy, as though both the past and the future are endlessly the same. I know now why Walter Benjamin, who was brought up in Berlin, time and time again describes a bitter experience as like someone driving a road straight through his heart. The series of notes that form the canonical *One-Way Street* is dedicated to a woman 'who as an engineer cut it through the author'. Sometimes I like to turn corners and feel I've left the past behind me.

But I don't want to turn a corner on Berlin for a while. It too cut through me like a silver knife, or rather a surgeon's scalpel that cuts to heal. I came back feeling a stronger, slightly more serious person. I was stopped in my tracks several times by the utter selflessness of the people I met. Yet all too soon the feeling began to evaporate, particularly on the ferry back from the Hook of Holland. It was an overnight ferry. In the duty-free shop a thousand spirit bottles rattled systematically in their metal racks, as if in the grip of some giant shaking hand. A kind of music for glass. Elsewhere one could be lulled into a fairyland by the gentle siren songs of video games as they chanted their little metallic mantras as they went down. There was a third-division heavy metal band out of their heads in the bar, or at least four leather-clad examples of England's finest well into their second bottle of brandy, playing cards and shouting 'Fucking cunt!' to each other every other minute. England arise, for the long, long night is over. London is calling. London calling!

II March 1989

For an outsider, the great thing about visiting the 'actually existing' socialist countries, is that the lack of shops, consumer goods, bars, restaurants, neon lights and crowded streets concentrates the mind wonderfully. The minimalism of the physical environment, and the lack of material distractions, helps people get to the point quickly. Within five minutes of sitting down people want to talk about whether the planet will survive or not, will the productive forces unleashed by capitalism outstrip the natural world's ability to meet global rising expectations, and will Gorbachev successfully defend *perestroika*?

I have been in East Berlin again, for a five day visit, including another seminar on 'Working-class writing in England and Ireland in the 1930s'. These people at the Humboldt University in the Unter den Linden are now old friends. Since I last went there, several of them have been to stay with us in London, in each case their first trip to the West. The conference is more a four-yearly reunion of about 30 academics and enthusiasts from the GDR, Soviet Union, the Federal Republic and Britain. This time it was held in the club room of a large youth centre in the new suburbs, where giant factories blow smoke across the new multi-storey flats on vast housing estates and the whole expanse of sky and concrete is woven together by pylons and tram-lines. Everything is covered in a fine dust. They are not learning from the mistakes of the West about re-housing and zoning, but seem to be painstakingly repeating every textbook disaster about how not to plan for people and human sociability and community. Up go the tower blocks, up go the factories, and the whole lot is run through with vast dual carriageways, tram-lines and railway services.

Perhaps the most incredible thing about this half of Berlin is that it has the most perfect transport infrastructure I've ever seen – buses, trams, U-Bahn, S-Bahn, railways, motorways, fast, reliable and astonishingly cheap – and nothing for the system to serve except the morning and evening rush hour between work and home. A case of all dressed up and nowhere to go. The transport system in East Berlin alone could probably service the whole of southern England, and yet for most of the time the roads are empty, and the housing estates and town centres are as quiet as ghost towns. The sadness of it all makes one weep.

They planned a minimum of pubs in the new housing districts because of drunkenness and now lots of people get completely blotto at home. You would think planners might occasionally talk to each other. Friday night shopping in the supermarket near the flat where I stayed was instructive. Plenty of meat, cabbage, bread, beer and spirits but little fruit or fresh vegetables. The people I stayed with kindly saved some oranges bought before Christmas for my visit. (When Isobel had stayed with us last summer she could not believe that there were so many different kinds of vegetables and fruit all year round.) They have tomatoes in the GDR – in September. And oranges at Christmas, just like during the war. Yet in a way they are at war; the feeling that the West still harbours aggressive intentions towards the countries of the Eastern bloc is no party-inspired paranoia. It is genuinely felt.

We went to the *Kaufhalle* (supermarket) on Friday night, along with thousands of other people, in the family Trabant car. I have told you about these before; they fascinate me. Trabants make Ladas look like Rolls Royces in comparison. I was told quite seriously that the bodies are made of wood pulp, but the trimmings are metal. Basically there is no other car available, so you can imagine what happens when you go to fetch your car from the 2000-place car park in front of the Hall of Socialist Culture in Alexanderplatz and there are 1999 other cars looking exactly the same.

People talk quite openly about every issue under the sun; they watch West German TV and books coming in from other countries are no longer intercepted at the post office. Well, not everybody watches western TV. There is a small part of East Berlin blocked by high rise flats and factories which cannot receive a TV signal from the West, and is known locally as 'The Valley of the Unenlightened'. But still a formidable bureaucracy rules. I filled in at least four different permission-to-stay cards, as well as being required to get two visas, one in Britain and another one at the local police station. The very physical fabric of the border crossing-point at Friedrichstrasse Station is a nightmare. Long queues shuffle into lock-gate type kiosks with a door at each end, one of which cannot open while the other is open, and there stern-faced officials with guns, sitting at sealed desks well above standing height, look down at you wordlessly while they pass your passport between them. There are mirrors, dogs and guns everywhere.

I've now realised what makes East Berlin look so particularly dowdy: they never seem to wash the windows of the shops and public buildings. You sometimes see this effect in Britain where a parade of shops has been left unlet and the filth on the windows quickly gives a feeling of neglect; in East Berlin this appearance is permanent, so that it is impossible to tell from the outside whether any building is open or closed. (Sometimes it's impossible to tell that even once inside.) For example, the large Museum of German History, which is full of interesting and important material (and some fairly major omissions), has its door closed all the time. Two great wooden doors with massive iron hinges, and they remain closed permanently. You have to literally force your way into the museum. And woe betide you if you forget to close the door behind you. Inside there is no sense of welcome, just a desultory and officious set of attendants servicing the main ideological storehouse of this new experiment in world history.

In the GDR, I was told on many occasions, public servants are kings; everybody is terrified of and defers continuously to museum attendants, shop-workers, waiters, town hall officials, and anybody else in a service role. Progressive really one might think, but it doesn't work that way. For it is clear that everybody is miserable. The waiters who refuse to look at you and leave you standing waiting for permission to sit down – I am not joking – cannot change jobs or pack it in. In the GDR unemployment is a crime. They are stuck in their jobs and it doesn't matter whether they do them well or badly – it's all the same. Some, of course, do them well, but it's totally random. Eating out is cheap but it's an emotional and psychological minefield. One evening, five of us went out to a restaurant on a new housing estate near where we were staying. The restaurant is in the basement of one of the tower blocks and has no signs advertising its presence outside. You enter a basement door as if going to see the caretaker and through another door you find yourself in a very pleasant 1950s restaurant. The staff are friendly, but they take their time. Opposite you a middle-aged couple are obviously celebrating a wedding anniversary or even a second marriage; anyhow, something important between them. They hold hands a lot. Her meal arrives half an hour before his. She has finished her meal, they have drunk the wine and still his meal hasn't arrived. Finally it does, they order some more wine, and then remind the waitress of the order. The wine arrives half an hour after he has finished his meal. And yet the restaurant is nearly empty and it is Saturday night.

On another occasion, on the last evening of the conference, fifteen of us decide to meet for a meal. The first to arrive are told that they can't order wine until they order their food; but, they explain, they are waiting for the others. Tough. They wait with nothing to drink. The others arrive, orders are made, and then over the next two hours food arrives in fits and starts. Mostly the orders are wrong, but no matter. At one point the waiter arrives with three plates, in the middle of a heated discussion about democratic centralism or something like that, and shouts at the party to shut up! He is about to serve some food and would they please listen! The bottle of wine I order, and which I remind the waiter several times about, arrives at the end of the evening, hours after the food. Perhaps this seems trivial, but our hosts fume and rage and boil within. Life is like this every day they say. We cannot break the bonds that hold us locked in these futile wars; everybody feels trapped and so they take it out on each other. At the university the porter often doesn't bother to tell our friends that books we have sent them have arrived; sometimes they are left outside in the rain. There are few personal or corporate loyalties beyond personal friendship. Shop-workers are often to be found shouting at customers who have got into a muddle about something, almost enjoying the public humiliation and embarrassment caused. This is no way to run a railway, let alone a country.

People do learn to live with these tribulations, although I fear they have learnt to defer to authority rather too well. One Saturday afternoon I was on my way to my favourite cemetery in the whole world – in Chaussee Strasse, where Brecht, Helen Weigel, Hans Eisler, Hegel, Fichte, John Heartfield, Anna Seghers and Paul Dessau are buried, among others – and I found myself surrounded by a crowd of young men, blowing whistles. I realised I was in the middle of a football crowd going to the match. They looked exactly like football supporters in England – faded denim jeans, jackets, training shoes and spotty faces – and they were pretty drunk as well, singing 'Here we go...' or rather, 'Hier wir gehen, hier wir gehen, hier wir gehen!' There were more police on the streets probably than at the fall of Berlin. Yet the lads blew whistles at them and mocked their officiousness. I thought, well things are looking up, at least they're taking the piss out of the police. And then what do they do? Hundreds of them bouncing down the empty street – the traffic had been diverted – and they come to a green man traffic sign and stop! And spend the next two minutes completely seriously waiting for the pedestrian light to change – and not a sign of a car anywhere.

And what of the conference? Well it was marvellous, again as I have stressed, because people don't pose, or waffle, or use the platform to advance their own careers. Even in the GDR the subject of working-class culture is regarded as slightly suspect; the serious intellectuals work on Shakespeare and Keats, as in Britain. Lip service only is paid to the assumption that I think most of us share, which is that cultural politics widens the possibilities of all other kinds of politics. Three particular 'moments' were extraordinary, when you felt that you were witnessing an exchange of ideas that actually might change the political worlds in which people lived. The first came when one of the British speakers, then unknown to me or Andy, gave a good account of Flora Thompson's *Lark Rise to Candleford* – with many profuse acknowledgements to Rebecca O'Rourke's work – but made frequent allusions to the Althusserian disappearance of the Subject, the Foucauldian thesis on the disappearance of the Narrative, Pierre Machery's thesis of the death of the Author, and an infinite regression of other *petits morts.* I tend to regard over-theorising with impatience, not so much because of the ideas, but because of the failure to articulate them in ways that most people can understand. There was a great debate because the socialist comrades had heard about these people and only faintly understood them. Then Gustav Klaus from the Federal Republic spoke, amusingly but seriously I thought, when he warned against too much 'disappearance of intentionality' in writing.

That was one moment. The second came at the end of a session I was chairing in which one contributor had given a rather pedestrian account of a documentary book written by an American woman visiting Russia in the 1930s, rather dully recounting the plot in the vein of, 'After that she visited the Lenin Path Tractor Collective where she was upset to find...', the point of the contribution being that some literature had seen through Stalinism at the time. At the end of the paper – which was at the end of a long day – there was a tired and leg-stretching silence. Then a colleague from the Institute of World Economy in Moscow spoke.

He was unhappy. The contributor seemed to be saying that all the problems of the socialist countries were Stalin's fault. There was no doubt that in world historical terms, Stalin was a tyrant of the greatest order. But now everybody was blaming everything on one man. Would the German comrades perhaps like to think a little more about certain historical/cultural pre-conditions that had made both Nazism and Stalinism possible? Shouldn't we all be a little more self-critical? What was it about the organisational forms, the hierarchies, the party structures that we had all complied with that had made Stalinism and Nazism possible? Were we yet entirely free of them? Did he not detect a certain feeling amongst the German comrades that they were blaming their present plight on the Russians when they had a few skeletons in their own cupboard too?

For a few seconds you could have cut the atmosphere in the room with a knife. Chairing the session, a hole opened up beneath my feet. It was five minutes to six and we had to be out by six. Yet to blithely close the conference for the day by saying something anodyne such as 'Well, thank you for that very interesting point; perhaps it's something we can think over while we are having our supper,' was not on. However, one of the most well-versed dialecticians from the GDR representatives, a Scots folk-singer who had moved to the GDR in the 1950s, gave a very clear and convincing acknowledgement of the issues raised that both recognised shared blame whilst at the same time rescuing the Soviet/GDR alliance in the post-war years. The conference relaxed, others made small contributions, but the issue had been raised and not swept away, and here I knew we were sitting in a room where people really could discuss everything.

The last moment was the most utopian. It came when the two women organisers of the conference who run the 'project' on working-class literature, explained during the last session the next stage of the work. There was to be a new emphasis – on contemporary women's writing and feminist theory. This, they felt, was a natural progression from the study of working-class writing in the 1930s, the last time an oppressed literature sought to totalise the political world. In their opinion women's literature today was the most advanced literature being written, which universalised the conditions and contradictions of society, and which sought to articulate the most fundamental form of oppression and exploitation now in existence. (I cannot express it in any way as well and as movingly as Isobel did.) Some of the men bridled and then fought back. 'Are we to assume that the project has now dispensed with that most fundamental of all forms of oppression – class – and has decided to ignore the continuing role of class struggle as the engine of progress towards a communist society in favour of a certain kind of petit-bourgeois writing about sex and other middle class issues?' The women replied, to the effect that in the current grave political situation in which the very future of the human species is under threat, then, in their opinion, it is women's literature which raises more social and political issues than any other kind of literature, and therefore is the most progressive literature being written today. Women's literature is now the universalising literature of humankind! They carried the day.

Four years before, as I knew from personal experience, the two women who achieved this enormous triumph themselves characterised feminist literature as 'diversionary'. Now there is an air of excitement about feminist literature and theory that is astonishing. The younger women students have taken over the project completely. And the older women teachers are in full support.

The city is still a rather scary landscape. The older buildings are pock-marked with bullet-holes and shrapnel scars from the ferocious fighting during the last weeks of the Russian encirclement. The new wide roads and monolithic office blocks and tower blocks lack character or human scale. It is a city of flags, plinths, statues and monuments. At night the streets are mostly empty. But change is in the air, I am sure. When Gorbachev makes a major speech the daily papers are sold out by breakfast-time. His every word is scrutinised for coded messages of hope. At the youth centre bar on the last night, the young people in their ersatz Benetton clothes and with drinks in their hand stand at the side of the dance floor, listening to a record of The Smiths singing 'Ask', the driving, hypnotic beat bouncing off the walls and into the cloakrooms. And I stand at the bar, too, breathing it all in and breathing it all out again. Nothing is really very different, not like I used to think it was. One minute I'm over there sitting on a seat by the Brecht statue enjoying the afternoon sun, next minute I'm back in this upstairs room writing this.

Within six months the wall was down and the experiment in history was over.

9 Krakow – Budapest September 1990

This summer I cycled from Krakow to Budapest, from Poland to Hungary, crossing the width of Czechoslovakia as well. The weather was fine, verging on the impossibly hot: on the last day we cycled 80 miles across the Hungarian wheatfields and plains in temperatures in their mid-90s; happily all Hungarian villages contain large numbers of bright-blue water hydrants in the street which can be pumped to provide eruptions of cold drinking water, which can also be used to dowse one's head, body and feet. Tomatoes, grapes and watermelons were available from roadside stalls as well. The body became a water recycling machine; solids were rarely bothered with during the daytime: water, tea, water, melon, yoghurt, water, sardines, water, grapes, melon and tea. And still thirsty. In the evenings we drank beer.

Yet unlike earlier rides this could never really be considered a holiday, for the landscapes we crossed, the towns and villages we passed through, still carried an air about them of a bitterly fought territorial past: of constantly changing borders and customs, of appropriation and re-appropriation, of oppression and resistance, of occasional victory but more often defeat. This was not a landscape to be used as a backcloth to an open-air reverie or social jaunt; this was a cycle ride through a still unresolved battleground. We started at Auschwitz.

Oswiecim (the Polish name), is just over 30 miles from Krakow and a number of us agreed that the day we had to spend in Krakow waiting for the bikes to arrive by lorry should be spent in part visiting the site of the wartime concentration camp. Not to have done so, while being so near, seemed an even more difficult decision than to simply get on the bus and go. We all felt a magnetic compulsion drawing us to go; and in a sense Auschwitz represents the negative pole of all twentieth century world history. It is where the era of the age of reason and the modernising and rationalising principle went horribly wrong. It was genocide planned and carried out on Taylorist principles. Instead of mass production it was a factory system planned and organised for mass extermination. It is a definitive twentieth century world shrine.

A teacher who was with the small party of us who made the visit said, 'It doesn't matter what we feel or say or try to comprehend; our feelings are irrelevant.' And that was the case; millions of tears of regret or remorse or anger don't change a single thing. It happened and there is nothing we can do about that. Yet as one was shown round the camp in the back of one's mind was a kind of feeling that it could all be made well again; rescued from time; the clock put back and everybody saved. Nonsense of course.

The first unsettling experience is that Oswiecim is still a working town. The extermination camp is simply one of a number of small factory sites in the immediate vicinity, many of which are still working. It reminded me of an industrial estate in Enfield, particularly the Ordnance Survey factory there, which is also comprised of a number of sturdy, redbrick sheds behind wire fences. This was no isolated fastness or grim prison impossibly sequestered on the moors or in the mountains; this was Unit 4 on the local industrial estate sharing all the same service roads and railway sidings. The unreality of that first impression only deepened.

The guide we had impressed us all. A young Polish woman in her late twenties, she spoke in a matter of fact, unemotional but commanding voice that told the whole terrible story as if it had only just happened. We were taken to the prison barracks, the punishment blocks, the kitchens, the wash-houses and the crematorium ovens. Many of the barracks had been converted into exhibition spaces where one might be shown a room-sized glass-fronted display cabinet just containing a mountain of suitcases piled high and deep, all with names and numbers scribbled on them by their past owners; or a room full of toothbrushes stretching endlessly towards the ceiling, or a room of artificial limbs, or a room containing thousands of pairs of old shoes. The millions of lives were represented by the items of personal clothing they left behind. Some barracks were lined with thousands of framed photographs of inmates staring into the camera (and therefore into the eyes of the visitor), with their length of stay (and therefore last days) officially recorded in ink below. Those I found the most upsetting; a good friend I made on the trip, a young Scots doctor, broke down when directed to a cabinet containing blankets made from human hair. In the end, however, what affected me most were the occasional bunches of fresh flowers, or single roses, laid in tribute on one of the gas oven doors or on a railway line junction point. Many of the visitors were Jewish. In Poland all schoolchildren are taken to Auschwitz at the age of fourteen.

From Auschwitz we were taken to Birkenau, just two miles away, the main extermination camp built as an annexe. This was a large camp set in farmland, comprising dozens of wooden stables sent unassembled from Germany where they were used to keep horses. (What was designed to stable 52 horses in Germany was used to accommodate 1500 prisoners in Poland.) It was at Birkenau that the majority of the four million who died were actually exterminated. 'The largest graveyard known to man,' said our guide, though two people in our guided tour probably did not hear her: a middle-aged Australian couple in Florida shorts who never looked out from behind the lens of their video camera, and who even filmed each other standing in front of the camp entrance with its infamous slogan *Arbeit Macht Frei.* We were all too flabbergasted at their behaviour to say anything. It was during this visit that I realised how often people use cameras or home videorecorders to distance themselves from actually seeing things.

We talked a lot about that visit during the next ten days; the memory of it kept floating to the surface of our minds from time to time, and it came up again and again whatever the conversation. I don't think we were immiserated by the experience; more disorientated. I think the strongest image that came to my mind was to do with darkness and the 'inlandness' of the excesses of the war fought in *Mitteleuropa,* in Poland, in Russia, in Germany, and which were best described in Primo Levi's novel, *If Not Now, When?*

On this journey, in which we cycled deeper into landlocked Europe, one sometimes longed for the breezes and fluidity of a coastline or an open sea. And in the way that all coastal climates are moderated by the sea, I felt that political and moral values might be tempered by the sea as well. The heat on the plains in Hungary, the landlocked Deep South in America, the inland voyage in Conrad's *Heart of Darkness* are all to do with the dangers and excesses of the interior. The sea always represents some kind of escape – or alternative. Auschwitz was a mire, excessively earthbound, fetid, a pit, a quagmire or a pyre – not when we visited it on a bright sunny day, but as the experience has come across in the memoirs of survivors. There was no fresh air; there was nowhere to run, not even to throw oneself into the sea to swim or drown. The watery element is where we come from; immersion is a baptism and a second chance. But not in the forested and asphyxiating interior. That was how I felt about it all.

Poland still seemed mesmerised. Static. Over-burdened by the past. In the villages along the road to Oswiecim, women and men cut the harvest in the fields by hand, with scythes and wooden rakes. The fields were full of serried rows of corn stooks like armies of occupation. On the roads there were as many horses and carts as there were lorries or cars. Many of the houses were traditional log-cabins, brightly painted with wells in the gardens still in use. And nobody smiled. In Poland it was impossible even to catch the eye or exchange a greeting with anybody over 40; they simply looked through us as if we didn't exist. Yet who could be more harmless than a cyclist on an open road? The children waved but the adults looked away. Or went back to tending the thousands of roadside and domestic shrines, almost exclusively devoted to the figure of Mary, the mother, never the son.

The cult of Mary, my Catholic doctor friend told me, took greatest root in peasant cultures. It appealed to the hard-working women in these societies and gave them a religious status – motherhood – that otherwise was denied. (Yet the minute we crossed the Czechoslovakian border the shrines reverted to the more familiar Crucified Christ.) Krakow was intensely religious, not surprisingly since their Bishop was chosen to be the current Pope. The town is myth-ridden I have to say. Every hour on the hour a trumpeter sounds a reveille from the main square church tower, recalling the brave trumpeter of the sixteenth century who alerted the people of Krakow to an impending attack and was struck by an arrow in the throat for his pains. The heroine of the town, Wanda, (we stayed in Hotel Wanda), is celebrated for her brave decision in the sixteenth century to throw herself into the River Vistula rather than marry a German, and the sentiments persist. Poland is the unhappiest of countries. First colonised by the Swedes, then the Czechs, then the Germans, it fought off the Turks at the end of the seventeenth century only to be colonised and divided up again by its neighbours, then the Nazis marched in and after that the Russians. The anti-Semitism of the Poles can perhaps be partly explained by the fact that there was never anybody else weaker to pick on; the Poles regard themselves as being at the bottom of the European pack, hated and derided by all their neighbours. But that doesn't explain everything, for these ancient hatreds still simmer in parts of Europe, where, as Conor Cruise O'Brien once said, 'anti-Semitism has always been a light sleeper.'

Krakow Cathedral, where all the Polish kings and queens are buried, is a baroque hallucination: dark, gloomy, florid murals and gigantic paintings of the stations of the cross in hideous gilt frames, effigies, marbled columns, stained glass, a riot of arches, columns, stairs, side-chapels, the religiosity it exemplified was distraught, guilt-ridden, oppressive, labyrinthine, tortuous and arcane. I hate baroque architecture and I hate the religious values it stands for. If you have to have religion let it be simple and light. Plain, unvarnished simplicity. This was cheap fairground art masquerading as the devotional; marble monumentalism not intended to lift the spirit to the skies but to crush it into the ground. The very touch and solidity of marble gives me the creeps. Thank god for fibre-glass, extruded plastic and stainless steel. It may look cheap but at least you know it won't last. We raised our vodkas in the square to provisional values. There can be few more chilling words in the dictionary than 'eternity'.

Quite quickly a group of us found ourselves with a lot in common, notably a relinquishing of old values – Communist, Catholic, Rationalist – together with a strong desire to find or establish something new. Significantly an interest in architectural styles, and the values they represent, emerged as a strong common thread; it's something in which I have become very interested, in recent years. Not just architecture but the whole of the visual and symbolic repertoire of the landscapes and built environments we live in or pass through. I don't know whether this is a common shift in middle age, but I have moved from a youthful pre-occupation with the wordy, the textual, the disputational as a source of values towards an appreciation of just how constructed and reconstructed we are by the visual world. That's why that spray of flowers on the crematorium oven door overwhelmed me, or why I feel that a certain kind of architecture – and even building material or ochre wash – can be either more liberating or oppressive than a manifesto or even an organisation. Or have I simply arrived at the door of the semiologists' convention 20 years too late?

So we discussed the Bauhaus, Czech car design, cultivated flowers, typefaces, house design and all the other visual references that made each village or town different from the next. Did you know that the reason Hitler hated the Bauhaus so much was that they favoured flat roofs, which he thought semitic in origin; he favoured roofs with steep pitches, gables almost reaching to the floor; the steeper the pitch the more essentially Germanic. Of such things are ideologies made and encumbered.

The Polish taxi-driver who brought us back from Auschwitz told us he knew only a little English: 'Hello. I love you. Goodbye.'

When we left Krakow on our bikes at the start of the ride we were given a police escort, though we had to keep giving the police motor bikes a push start as they were always stalling. It was raining when we left and we cycled out through the industrial suburbs which, like other Eastern bloc countries, brought back to me very strong memories of London in the early 1950s. Cobbled streets, tram-lines, horses and carts, piles of coal dumped in the streets at regular intervals, broken down shopfronts with filthy windows displaying the odd bar of soap, soft drink bottle, washing-up brush. Unmade roads, factory smoke blowing in all directions, lorries with no covers over the engines belching black smoke, and trains and tram-lines sharing equal rights of way across the roads. Did I really see this London or did I only see it on film? I think I did see it because when I was young I used to go with my father in his lorry during the school holidays, delivering and collecting loads of plywood from the London docks. We would call in at the steamiest of transport cafes where the cigarette smoke vied with the tea urn and the frying pan for producing the thickest clouds – a good fug, it was called. The condensation on the cafe windows made it impossible to see, in or out. The hissing and bubbling of the urn, the clash of the cutlery, the shouting and violent coughing was at times quite frightening. Jack Warner territory. My father, hard case though he was – and as heavy drinking and misogynistic as the rest – corrected anybody who swore in my presence. 'Do you mind, mate, there's children sitting here.' He cut a solitary figure in the proletarian crowd; in it but not of it; he struggled to avoid conformity all his life. And still does.

In a Krakow second-hand bookshop where I bought some very ornate old postcards, the staff spoke in the quietest of whispers, much quieter than the people in the cathedral. They had the same exaggerated hand movements when handling books or prints as one would find in a jewellers or a haute couture dress shop; literature still possesses a unique aura; books are still sacred.

We were careful what we ate in the more isolated cafes in the rural areas, always delaying a bit so that other cyclists up front were given time enough to order the soup, which sometimes turned out to be tripe or pig's feet. We could then order on the basis of their mistakes. A local delicacy I read in my guide book was *czarnina*, a black soup made from fresh pig's blood, bones, giblets and cherries. It was the idea of the cherries that put me off. Offal was and is so often the basis of the cafe midday soups. The sausages obviously contained everything, ears, eyes, nose and throat no doubt, but then so they do in Britain except we are more sophisticated and wash it from the carcasses with high-power hoses turning it into a kind of animal slurry or paste. Yes, Poland doesn't attempt to gild the lily or make a purse from a sow's ear. It eats it.

There were problems – and arguments back at camp – about the inflated currency we had to use. In Poland a pound gives you nearly 17,000 zlotys, so you can wave a bundle of notes in the air and still not have enough to pay for a cup of tea. For us it was monopoly money, yet the Poles were scrupulous in wanting small denominations to pay for things and scrupulous in giving change. I started the holiday with three large denomination notes and after days of spending ended up with more notes than I could carry. It was like the Midas touch, the more you spent the more money you seemed to end up with.

A few cyclists would offer up a 50p note for something that only cost 7p and leave the change behind, which of course was an insult and an act of gratuitous patronage. They couldn't be bothered to understand the value of the notes they had and just waved handfuls around. In the villages often a 25p note would be gently pushed back with a request for something smaller. We are talking about a country in which 50p is a large sum not to be treated lightly. In the camp at night some of the older or more hard-bitten cyclists would deride or berate the younger ones who made fun of the currency, often leading to quite bitter arguments. Seasoned (and often older) metropolitan or domestic values were openly ranged against 'yuppie' values and sentiments, ending in slanging matches or worse. These arguments clearly represented deeper cultural attitudes and moods. And although 'Yuppie' is hardly a term of sophisticated cultural analysis, it is interesting how much it flared up in private conversations as a term of deep abuse. Is it just our old friend class, or is it something generational and geographical as well?

Despite the poverty and the defensiveness, Poland is a country in love with flowers. Every peasant garden was emblazoned with gladioli, chrysanthemums, giant daisies, antirrhinums, roses, red-hot pokers, or sunflowers, in tremendous profusion; every roadside shrine was decorated with fresh flowers daily; in the towns and cities people were often seen carrying bouquets and single roses to give to one another. Happier surely is the country with more flowersellers than estate agents or burger bars. In the street markets there were as many flower stalls as food stalls.

In the fields we saw storks, and in some of the villages, storks' nests, amazing constructions, giant birds' nests, up to six feet in diameter, each balanced on top of the roadside telegraph poles like a plate on a conjurer's wand. A red squirrel ran out in front of me in Poland; in Hungary I pitched my tent beneath a tree in which in the morning a woodpecker tapped away quite happily in full view. But in general there was little other distinctive wild life which I managed to see, although we cycled through one of the Hungarian national parks where there were wild boar and possibly bears.

The last day in Poland was just a short ride, all over by lunchtime. We camped near the Czech border, and the weather was so lovely I went out for a ride on my own to the border on one of the very smallest of roads. It was an afternoon of sheer heaven. I had a good map, and the route I chose took me along a river valley for nearly 15 miles, with only a few hills to climb. Alongside the river ran a railway line; the valley floor was sparsely populated with fields, rising to broad-leaf forests and then mountains. The train and the river – one of the man-made environment's happier congruences. Coming back in the early evening the air was fresh and damp on my skin, the sun was beginning to cast shadows, and I was cycling along a smooth and empty road all the time staying close to the river; it can't be beaten. The bike sailed along almost effortlessly; there were no intimations of mortality at all in any of my senses. It doesn't happen every day.

Crossing the border from Poland into Czechoslovakia meant cycling up, into, and through the Tatra Mountains. These are as spectacular and lovely as the Pyrenees or the Picos De Europa. But already the developers and investors are moving in, with hundreds of new ski flats and hotels being built in anticipation of tens of thousands of more tourists from the West. Hitherto most of the tourists to the Tatras have been from the GDR and from my experience of that country and its people they would not have been particularly prone to driving BMWs, leaving litter everywhere, vandalising the toilets or wrecking the town. More likely they would have dusted the footpaths as they went. All this will change.

In Czechoslovakia (or Slovakia as the locals properly insisted we call it), the roads were new and empty; ideal for those long descents through the pine forests and into the valleys. And as soon as we came into farming land again we cycled alongside vast wheatfields that stretched for miles in all directions, with dozens of combine harvesters in rows moving across the landscape and disappearing over the horizon like mechanical toys. This was collectivised farming with a vengeance: agri-business that left not a single topographical feature in its wake. At times it was like a moonscape. We were glad to get through that.

In Slovakia too we found that many of the villages not only still had public PA systems with loudspeakers strung along the street and hanging from the church walls, but they were frequently playing pop music or announcing local fairs. Our first night in Slovakia was spent on a campsite near Lavoco, a town I'd never heard of then but will never forget now. That night, after a big collective evening meal in the campsite restaurant, and entertainment from a live folk band, I left the hall early feeling tired and in need of an early night. We were still in the High Tatras, and, negotiating my way through the tent pegs and ropes, bicycles and dustbins, I became conscious of the most dazzling night sky, more brilliant than one I witnessed in the Pyrenees. The stars were countless, some as big as dinner plates; the milky way was almost palpable, a great swathe of shimmering silver light across the sky. And then I involuntarily thought of Auschwitz and suddenly felt a dagger to the heart and a sense of utter incomprehension and extremity. I stood there for a minute not knowing what to think, bit my lip, and crawled into the tent to sleep. In the morning, of course, all the confusion had gone.

The next day we passed through Lavoco, perhaps a typical Slovakian town and indescribably beautiful, very much in the architectural style of the Austro-Hungarian tradition and a taste of the beautiful city Prague which I have still yet to see. Naturally there was a large town square with the town hall and main church in the middle. The church contained the largest altar in the world and was full of ornate gilded paintings, fantastic carvings of the disciples at the last supper, dozens of side chapels and endless arrangements of flowers. But the best thing was the square, full of seventeenth and eighteenth century buildings, all with elegantly painted fronts, patterned and stencilled in golds and browns on pink and other pastel washes, with dozens of tiny shuttered windows in each façade; every house in the square looked like an advent calendar. It was a Saturday morning and people were busy shopping, talking, buying flowers, cycling in the square. Resistance to the Nazi occupation had been fierce in this region; the Slovakians are like the Basques, a distinct and self-contained people.

What do we mean by good company? On this ride more than any other – and it has always been a terribly important feature of these journeys (or secular pilgrimages) – I have made friendships and enjoyed people's company in ways that just don't happen in everyday life. And mostly they only last for the duration of the trip. There are a few postcards and Christmas cards in the months that follow; and occasionally a meeting up on other rides. But for the time itself, the friendships, conversations, running jokes, sheer pleasure of coming across newly familiar faces on the cafe stops, or sitting together at the same table of an evening is overwhelmingly important. A doctor whom I've met on several rides told me that a group of 14 who cycled in China three years ago – and who hadn't known each other before – still meet up three times a year because of the closeness the group developed on the ride. A group cycling trip involves an intense social life, a year's worth of parties and social events squeezed into 14 days. One is endlessly finding oneself sitting at odd cafe tables, outside bars, on walls alongside a watermelon seller, in bus shelters if it is raining, at the dinner table or bar at night, in various combinations from the same group of people. It is like a cafe society on wheels. A *fin de siècle* culture – Vienna, Dublin, Greenwich Village – in lurex shorts and a change of cities or even countries every evening. Changing countries more often than we changed our shoes, as Brecht put it describing an unhappier period of travel across Europe.

Hungary just kept getting hotter. Small shops are now beginning to be displaced by supermarkets; the village butchers and bakers are already on their way out it would seem. And then we came to the Danube. The only book I took on holiday was Claudio Magris' *Danube*, a long political travelogue of a journey down the Danube in 1988 recording the decline of the great Ottoman, Austro-

Hungarian and Soviet communist empires. It is a wonderful book, and some parts moved me to tears, because Magris continues to recognise some of the genuine strengths and possibilities that had once been contained in the communist ideal: internationalism, egalitarianism, exemplary public behaviour. The best chapter is a short set of reflections on the Karl-Marx Hof, the famous workers' flats built in the 1930s in Red Vienna. They exemplified what at the time were the best values available: modernisation, dignity and equality in housing, human solidarity. We might hold different values now – in many things – but Magris is anxious that we don't throw the better part of that austere tradition away in a welter of postmodernist relativity. OK, says Magris, we are ideological orphans; but everybody has to lose their parents some time. You respond to the new conditions but you don't deny the past. I still long for an intellectual, disciplined, activist political culture of the left, but perhaps that's an impossible dream.

In my work these days I drown daily in a turgid sea of political imprecision, jargon and incoherence: partnerships, coalitions, development trusts, action programmes, empowerment courses, capacity building strategies and leadership training; endless quangos are set up to mystify local political decision-making even more, a miasma of post party-political alliances that everybody is suddenly too embarrassed to contest, but which haven't achieved a single thing in giving people's lives more dignity and self-respect at all. (They haven't even built a single new house in many towns, and a new school is a thing of the past. But can modern professionals talk and write reports.) The one thing I always admired about many of the Communist Party members I have known – from all walks of life – was that they possessed a sense of their own usefulness and agency, and that they believed others could too. I want that back. Please. And I want the language of modernisation and planning back as well. We live in such a political culture of short-termism that even to talk of next year in some quarters is to produce open-eyed and quizzical surprise. Nobody believes in the future anymore, but how can you possibly carry on without lifting your eyes beyond next week? Maybe they should make 50 year Filofaxes. Forward with the great five-year contingency plan. Forward with the heroic three month interim report!

The trip could not have ended better. At the end of the longest – and last – day, the 80 mile journey involved two short ferry rides across the wide and dazzling Danube: across and back again to cut a corner. We went from one pretty riverside baroque town to the next. From one amazing ice-cream kiosk to another. We camped in Szentendre, drank our celebratory pink champagne, loaded our bikes into the van, re-assembled for the last time at the camp restaurant that evening, sang a medley from Showboat, and went to bed. In the morning, already 80 degrees by 9am, most of us took the hour and a half boat ride down the Danube to Budapest.

Our first sight of Budapest from the river left many of us open-mouthed. Magris describes it as a solid city of outdated futurism, like the city in *Bladerunner* or an Islamic version of Chicago: it is heavy, grid-built, fortress-like, and fronted by the most Gothic of parliament buildings I've ever seen; 1950s modernist communist-type hotels rise up behind granite waterfront administration buildings; squares with heroic statues in them are entered into from poor tenement streets. I liked it a lot I must say, but we were only there for a few hours.

On the principle that if you only have a few hours in a large city then best do just one thing, some of us decided to spend most of the time in the fabled Gellert Hotel Turkish Baths. This vast, art deco complex of swimming baths, thermal baths, sulphur baths, massage rooms, saunas, would be pretty frightening if you were on your own. For it is a subterranean labyrinth of unmarked rooms and corridors, bells to be rung, doors to be waited at, towels to be collected and disposed of, and so on. We had a swim, a sulphur bath, a massage and another swim outdoors. There was a list of services and facilities at the entrance that reached well over a hundred different options, including acid baths, mud massages, and others. The only thing we couldn't hire were stick-on walrus moustaches, without which we felt somewhat naked in the sulphur baths, swishing around in the hot, stinking murky waters, surrounded by men with magnificent moustaches. We took the spirit of Budapest in through our pores.

That night we took the train back to where we had started, from Budapest to Krakow, and spent most of the time eating, drinking and talking in the furtive atmosphere of a Russian train compartment. In one compartment the band played their acoustic instruments, people mixed in the corridors as if at an expensive cocktail party; the whole thing was like a scene from *Some Like It Hot.* Flea-bitten, hot and tired, people fitfully slept.

10 Brisbane – Melbourne – Perth September 1988

Earlier this year I was invited to go to Australia to speak at the Second National Conference on Writing and Publishing in the Community in Melbourne. Upside down? No, not really, just eerily moon-like from an aerial view of the landmass which I flew across in daylight for several thousand miles, before arriving in Sydney and changing planes for Brisbane, later crossing the complete width of the continent to Perth, and finally flying home along the east coast for, literally, hours in brilliant sunshine, and so cloudless that at 35,000 feet we could still see the waves beating on the barren shore.

Australia is not another country, it is another planet. Its landscape is unique, its birds and animals are unique, and it is a tropical south-east Asian continent that is run and administered as though it were North Finchley. I mean where else would you close the curtains in a small suburban residential district at night that looks and feels just like Brookside Close, only minutes later – as darkness fell – to hear the agonised screamings and blood-curdling howls of giant parrots, kookaburras, and various other creatures of the night demanding to be let back into the jungle. It is also a tragic landscape. The first European colonists never understood it and the dominant theme in Australian painting is the continuing attempt to try to represent the landscape outside of European conventions and traditions. People still disappear frequently, getting lost and dying within a few dozen yards of such roads as there are in the interior. Today large mining and timber corporations happily burn or cut down the remaining rain forests, feeding rare mahoganies and other hardwoods into wood-chip machines to make up blockboarding for laminated kitchen furniture. The only people who understand the landscape, the Aboriginals, have been driven off it and into the cities to live on welfare and drink themselves to an early death in car parks and on pieces of vacant wasteland. Not a happy story.

'Here's a key, here's a map, just come and go as you want. We'll all be in the Boundary Bar at 6, the show's at 7.30, we usually have a Lebanese meal afterwards, and as it's Friday we usually go round someone's house and sit out on the deck and have a few beers. By the way, this is Harvey, this is George, this is Melanie, this is Mike: we all live in each other's houses, it's pretty informal round here. You can wash in here, the shower works like this, don't worry about the cockroaches they don't bite, there's usually some beer in the fridge, the local deli's just round the corner, keep clear of the cat at the moment, she's got fleas, the community radio station is on 83.8 FM. If a strange bloke comes round looking for Melanie say she went to Sydney last week. The TV only works on two stations and you have to kick it. Any clothes you want to wash, there's a sink and stuff in the basement. Keep the back door locked when you go out, and if you hear arguing next door it's a hostel for alcoholics – it's upsetting at first but you get used to it. If you want to go into town you get the 81 bus just before the Freeway. I'll leave a list of phone numbers of people just in case you get stuck. The Carrot Cafe's not bad if you want a snack, that's just on the main drag. I wouldn't bother going to Expo if I was you. The city museum's dreadful but there's a good exhibition of Aboriginal painting on at the main gallery. Avoid the shopping mall if you don't want to be brain-damaged. The Botanical Gardens are lovely, see you later!' The woman who had kindly met me at the airport and put me up in her home, then left me to my own devices while she went back to community organising.

So I spent my first afternoon in Australia in Brisbane, avoiding the World Expo, sitting in the art gallery gardens drinking coffee, writing postcards, and watching the extraordinary birds which came and went in the grounds and gardens. Then back to the 'West End' where I was being looked after so solicitously. The 'West End' is a neighbourhood of handsome, if ancient, wooden bungalows on stilts, each with a front or rear verandah where people sit out and drink, play chess and chat. It's being run down in the interests of property speculation and rising land values associated with the arrival of Expo. It's a kind of suburban Notting Hill. It has a main drag, Boundary Road, one street of garish filling stations, drive in banks, radical bookshops, discount shoe shops, all with windows full of day-glo posters – 'Today! 10 lb Porterhouse Steak only $80!' – that kind of thing. And it has the Boundary Hotel. The name Boundary Street indicates that that was as far as Aboriginals were allowed to go into Brisbane, right up until the Second World War. It was only the arrival of black GIs that broke down this extraordinary geographical and racial barrier. Until then, the blackfellas – as they proudly call themselves – weren't allowed across the river and into the city.

OK. The Boundary Hotel. Now I was looking forward to my first visit to a real Australian bar, but I wasn't expecting anything so rough and functional as I found. I thought I'd have a mid-afternoon drink before heading back to where my bags were being kept, but at the door of the bar I lost my nerve and crept away. The main bar looked like a cross between an empty meat-packing shed and a massage parlour, decorated in the style of a mini-cab office in Finsbury Park – black painted walls, ripped plastic seats, dirty lino floor, a television in one corner, and the customers in shorts, torn vests, plimsolls, and sporting beer bellies that reached down to where their shorts finished. Never has a bar looked so devastatingly uninviting. Yet later that evening everybody in 'the community' was down there, in the back bar, as if it was home from home. But people weren't just in the back bar: others were standing and chatting in the bottle shop (off-licence), whilst others were queuing up in their cars for the drive-in service, everybody yelling across the bars, through open car windows, across the off-licence counter, about where the party was going to be, where people would be eating later, who would join in a shout to buy a bottle of Irish whiskey. Suddenly I realised where I'd seen this small town Friday night scene before; I was taking part in a grown up version of *American Graffiti* or *Diner*. And that's exactly how it was. People were constantly jumping in and out of each other's cars to get to the show, to get to the restaurant, to go back to the Boundary Bar, to collect some records from Mike's, to fetch some extra glasses from Melanie's, and so on. I hadn't lived like this since I was a student, and then we didn't have cars.

The show that everybody was going to see wasn't bad, a community theatre production based on workshops with local working-class white and aboriginal women about domestic life, but as far as the audience was concerned it was the greatest thing since the development of guild drama. People whooped as each character came on stage or soliloquised for more than 20 seconds, hugged each other with delight at every joke; the audience, as they say, was very supportive. The show was done on a makeshift stage in the community arts centre which itself was an abandoned bowls club building. People chain-smoked throughout the play and afterwards everybody helped dismantle the set and load it and the hired chairs into a fleet of old vans and station wagons before heading off back to the Boundary Hotel again.

It was the women who made the running everywhere, and were known locally as 'the Femocrats'. The lads did exactly what they were told. Later on that night, still my first day in Australia and still not having slept properly for two days, sitting out on the verandah chatting and smoking, the boys decided to go out for a day in the bush the next day and invited me to join them. Saying goodnight to the crowded veranda and the dozens of empty bottles (dead soldiers) I managed to get my first night's sleep dreaming of crows with white wings. Very soon afterwards Harvey, Mike and George, so it seemed, were knocking at the door with their bags full of avocado or asparagus and vegemite sandwiches, asking Pat if I could come for a trip out to the bush.

We drove into some hills about 60 miles away where there was still some rainforest remaining and we walked about ten miles through the forest, to the top of the hills and back down again. On the journey there Mike spotted an eagle in a tree and we parked the car within 20 yards of a bare tree in which a massive wedge-tailed eagle sat unconcerned by our presence. I have never been so close to such a bird before; it was the size of a small child, and when it finally took off and opened its wings it was like a magician's black cape suddenly unfolding and shutting out the sky. And in the forest the noises were deafening – parakeets, whip-birds, bell-birds – and brightly coloured bush turkeys came right up to us when we sat down to eat our sandwiches. And in the forest too, giant gum trees, flourishing vines and creepers trailing and looping everywhere, and ferns and palm-leaf type bushes in profusion. Before the war some Aboriginals would still have been living here as hunters and bush-dwellers; that's how astonishing and extraordinary is the nature of the uneasy co-existence between a residual 'primitive' culture and the suburban European culture of the white Australians.

The views from the hills were wonderful, the rain clouds moving between the valleys like smoke, the empty landscape wherever you looked, the tropical vegetation and the mesmerising calls of the birds. The only thing was that, unknown to me at the time, I got bitten by a rather vicious insect, probably a kangaroo tick. Three days later, in my hotel room in Sydney, I became conscious that my scalp had gone completely numb and that there was a large bump on the back of my head. A day later feeling the bump again I felt something slimy sticking to my head. A day later, gathering courage in the shower, I pulled it off, a small oyster shaped thing, now headless because that's what they leave behind. Apparently they can kill babies or dogs in extreme circumstances, but three weeks later the bump's still there and my scalp tingles but I'm still standing.

That night another party, another set of car cruises down Boundary Street, in and out of the drive-in bottle shop, and endless Elvis Costello records everywhere we went. The following day we drove to the beach, a short 60 miles each way, staying only for two hours when we got there, and that final evening I tried to repay the many kindnesses given to me by putting on a slide-show and a talk at the community arts centre. The following morning I crept out of my bed at 5am to wait for the taxi to take me to the airport to fly to Sydney. Dawn and the birds screaming and whooping in the trees, the taxi rising into view over the hilly street like a shot from *Bullitt*, me sorry to leave so soon, leaving behind a fairly rare surviving community that still stayed true to the spirit of the sixties, curiously innocent, curiously alive.

Sydney was very different. It is true that the harbour, the bridge and the Opera House together make up one of the most astonishing cityscapes in the world; on a bright day, with the sun bouncing off the water, Sydney Harbour makes Manhattan look dull and ordinary. And at night the effect is even more astonishing, particularly because of all the ferries and boats moving in and out of the various bays, quays and moorings. But political corruption and the unfettered ravages of endless property development seem to be turning the city into a featureless high-rise business district.

Sydney is the fast-talking, hard-living metropolis in Australia, the Chicago or Glasgow of Australia rather than the Boston or Edinburgh which Melbourne or Perth represent. And it houses Australia's tough-guy school of male writers, some of whom I met by chance at a literary bar and got introduced to, though I found their work which I read afterwards, pretty misogynistic, as if they had just discovered Henry Miller. They are all happy to denounce social workers, feminists, sandal-wearers, and so on, but themselves live off enormous government grants and fellowships which they sit on panels to award each other. Corruption – literary, political, economic – never travels in disguise in Australia; it's accepted as a fact of life.

Sydney had been the key site for the Bicentennial celebrations with the re-enactment of the arrival of the First Fleet into Sydney Harbour 200 years ago. But at the re-enactment in January something else had happened too: Aborigines from all over Australia had marched on the harbour, all carrying the distinctive red, yellow and black flag of the Land Rights Movement, with white Australian sympathisers following on behind, and this demonstration, very dignified, very large, had captured the television cameras and galvanised the nation. The politics of land rights is clearly one of the major issues now running through Australian society, and more and more I realised through many conversations, that the politics of 'place', whether of desert or of threatened suburb, of riverside community or rainforest tribe, is likely to be a much more important mobilising politics than class in the near future; certainly in Australia but increasingly in Britain too. People's wish to stay where they feel happiest is likely to come under greater and greater threat as international capital and the unregulated play of market forces move in on natural resources, or require the demolition of whole neighbourhoods for office or retail development.

One of the most interesting features of the rapid rise and effectiveness of the Aboriginal land rights movement was the invention and adoption of a national flag. A brilliant publicity device – a wonderful example of the invention of tradition – the flag is now to be seen everywhere, on murals, on badges, on posters, on cars, flying above wooden bungalows, uniting a whole set of issues, individuals, campaigns and organisations, under a common banner. The flag suddenly gave the whole issue a symbolic identity. And when the aborigines marched on Sydney Harbour, 'terrible as an army with banners', carrying thousands of those distinctive flags, then at last it dawned on white Australia that there was another people living in Australia too, with a flag of their own, and a rather longer tenancy. 40,000 years rather than 200 years in fact.

Three days in Sydney and a late night flight to Melbourne for the conference. Here they put me up in a motel near the centre of town and it was suddenly a relief to have a room of my own, completely private, even though I had enjoyed being put up in other people's houses. Melbourne is a fine city, having a very central European feel to it mainly because it has retained its network of trams, many of which are very old but very solid, with polished wooden interiors and brass rails. What is it about trams that seems so civic and sociable? And Melbourne has retained its elegant suburbs of nineteenth century close-packed bungalows, each ornately decorated with wrought-iron verandahs, balustrades, palm-tree gardens. There is something genuinely Edwardian about the city.

And Melbourne was of course the reason for my visit, and hence initially a source of some apprehension. After all, they had paid the airfare, a hotel bill and a fee for one opening 'keynote' speech; what if I fouled up? What if I forgot what it was I wanted to say? Or lost my voice? Or turned up at the wrong conference?

The day started unpropitiously. The mikes didn't work, they couldn't find the slide projector, but I soon realised that Australians are a lot less uptight about such things. (That's why they put 'community' in front of everything these days – it means take it easy.) And when the time came to put my sheet of paper on the lectern and smile at the audience and reach for the first word of what I wanted to say, everything luckily fell into place.

The whole of the first day of the conference was given over to the platform, and though the standard of speeches and contributions was high, I thought it rather tough on the audience and expected a mutiny at some point in the afternoon. But mutiny was there none. No one challenged the gender or racial balance of the platform, no one demanded additional workshops to cover topics not decided by the organising committee, no one set up caucuses or distributed lunchtime leaflets calling for the conference programme to be jettisoned in favour of a newer and more radical agenda. Everybody smiled, cheered, clapped and demurred appreciatively. Very tolerant and friendly audiences, I said to the organisers at lunch on the first day. Too bloody nice, the organisers replied. Why doesn't somebody denounce us for fuck's sake, or storm the platform or occupy the dining hall? Bloody community writers, bloody Australians, they'll go down smiling!

It was then that I began to realise there was a problem. Years of benign state funding for the arts, years of populist cultural rhetoric, decades of 'One Australia' classlessness, had made it genuinely difficult to develop an oppositional culture or politics. I would say that 95 per cent of the audience were currently in receipt of direct state funding as 'community writers', 'community theatre workers', paid arts administrators, development workers and so on. In Australia, it seems, all the radicals are on the payroll. So where do you go from there? For example – and this is only a minor exaggeration – a recent and bitter strike of timber workers in one of the New South Wales bush towns had led to a small exodus of community writers, community photographers and community theatre workers to head for the town to document the strike, take photographs of the strike, collect oral testimonies, develop playscripts and produce a community play about the event. Fine you might think. But the irony was that many of these activists had been indignant that it had taken weeks to get state and federal grants to travel north to do this work! The expectation that all cultural work should automatically get funding had created a highly integrated and incorporated political culture. People were amazed when I said that most of this kind of cultural activism in Britain was done for free.

The other problem I found had to do with definitions of writing. In Australia the writers' workshop movement has been established in the interests of professional writers and not primarily in the interests of widening the range of people writing. It is seen as a way of providing jobs and state funding for existing writers. So the definition of being 'a writer' in Australia is not to do with the quality of your work, its political impulse, its innovative qualities; it is to do with whether you can get a state grant to run a writers' workshop! State funding is the final legitimation that you are a writer.

One area of Australian cultural life where there clearly is a strong oppositional culture is in community radio. In Britain I was rather sceptical towards the community radio lobby which I found over-concerned with the potential sound of their own voices rather than with creating new communities and audiences. But the two stations I visited in Australia, 4ZZZ in Brisbane and 3CR in Melbourne had a very anarchic, independent, irreverent and iconoclastic feel to them. The Brisbane station had recently been accused of fomenting a prisoners' strike in the state as a result of their weekly prisoners' programme, and the Melbourne station had been accused of trying to start a civil insurrection when it rallied several neighbourhoods to oppose a new freeway planned to carve its way through a residential district. In the latter case, the station had broadcast daily morning bulletins as to where to gather to demonstrate, what the police were planning, which politicians had voted which way, and had successfully defeated a major piece of development chicanery.

In whichever city I was staying I tuned into the largest local community radio station and really very soon got a feeling for the city that no other medium, I now realise, can provide so well. The aboriginal programmes mixing country and western (the music of the Aborigines) with political comment, humour, announcements of meetings, poems, all in a very relaxed and direct style; the pensioners' programmes playing big band music, listing free events in town that day, recipes, dedications, items of local history and so on; the music programming which for both 4ZZZ and 3CR was self-regulated to play 40 per cent Australian music, including 30 per cent of all records to be by women; it's a whole different kind of radio. It is just so un-English to hear a wry radio presenter humorously but mercilessly unpicking every lie and innuendo in the daily newspapers or suggesting that it might be a good idea for senator so and so to do a few days work for a change, or enjoining people to get themselves organised for a particular forthcoming local struggle because 'as you all know, the politicians will sell you down the river as soon as look at you'.

3CR is entirely funded from individual subscriptions (80,000 of them) and donations. This gives them the independence from the state which enables them to be genuinely critical and iconoclastic. And here there were advantages to the fairly un-sectarian attitudes between 'communities of interest' in Australia which often dog such projects in Britain, because at 3CR every 'minority' group – gays and lesbians, Aborigines, trades unionists, pensioners – appeared to co-operate to provide each other with airtime, and worked alongside each other on the management of the station.

Finally then to Perth. I was slightly hesitant about the Perth part of the visit because I had already met the person I was to be staying with, in London, and had found him rather ponderous and vague, characteristics which annoy me, though I realise that is really my problem rather than other people's. Like many London intellectuals I over-value verbal fluency and a knowing wit: too clever by half, my father would sometimes say of me and my friends. Just words, words, words. Yet my would-be host was the person mostly responsible for getting me invited to Australia so I was certainly in his debt.

His name was Bryn Griffiths, a heavy, grey-bearded Welshman in his mid-fifties who had lived in Perth for a dozen years and worked for most of the time as a trade union officer. He was a writer himself, and on frequent trips back to Britain had become interested in the community writing and publishing movement there, and wanted to set up something similar in Western Australia, working with the unions. For four days I stayed at his bungalow, just four hundred yards from the Indian Ocean, and got to know him well and came to admire him enormously. He had been brought up in a very poor working-class family in Swansea, his father dying while Bryn was still young, and at 15 he had left school to join the Merchant Navy. During his teen years he had, in his own words, 'drunk a lot, fought a lot, read a lot – and then began to write.' I can imagine he must have been a pretty tough character at the time, as he still retained a stocky, athletic build. I believed his stories when he told me how on several occasions on the London literary scene – at poetry readings or parties – when some Oxbridge poet had mocked his Welsh accent Bryn had responded with a single blow, felling them to the ground. 'I can take most things, mind, Ken, but you can't have people taking the mickey out of the way you speak, can you? I just hit them.'

So after ten years at sea and a lot of union work, Bryn had gone to Coleg Harlech for a year, and from that adult education college had sent off a first collection of poems to London. Now at exactly this time the world was waiting for a new Dylan Thomas, and so the first publisher Bryn approached snapped up this first collection, published it and promoted him as the new Welsh poet for a new generation. It was actually quite a strong collection, as I discovered when I read it in his bungalow along with lots of his other published work. What happened next was that Bryn, like Byron before him, awoke one morning to find himself famous. This was right at the beginning of the 1960s. He moved to London, fell in with the Hampstead set, toured with Adrian Henri, Roger McGough and Brian Patten, gave endless readings in coffee bars and pubs, became close friends with B.S. Johnson and the actor Ronald Fraser, and ended up working as a scriptwriter at the BBC. He told me all this in the foreshore restaurant we used to go to every evening, and where we washed down barrimundi or John Dole fish steaks with bottles of Australian chablis. He moved me to tears with his account of working on the special Aberfan edition of *That Was The Week That Was*, when he had scripted and coached the actor Stanley Baker ('bit of a hard nut himself') into reading Idries Davies' great poem, 'Send out your homing pigeons, Dai', which he proceeded to recite aloud in the restaurant:

> Send out your homing pigeons, Dai,
> Your blue-grey pigeons, hard as nails,
> Send them with messages tied to their wings,
> Words of your anger, words of your love....

We agreed that Idries Davies remained one of the most important, but neglected poets, of the 1930s. So Bryn had had a good sixties. But after a while he, and others, realised he wasn't a new Dylan Thomas, that his poetry was uneven, and so his publisher dropped him, and the publishers who were interested in his work became smaller and smaller. He met a woman from Perth, married her, and moved to Australia. In recent years he had returned to seafaring again, working trips out of Fremantle, organising poetry competitions among the wharfies and seamen, and running a small press. I quickly grew to enjoy his diffident, slightly self-contained company.

The last day and a half I had completely to myself. The weather which had been stormy and rainy, turned to blue skies, a hot sun, and a dazzling clear, golden light which touched everything with a great luminousness. So on both mornings I got up early and walked down to the beach, past the local off-licence which called itself 'The Liquor Library', past the cycle shop and the butchers, past the bank, across the sand dunes and on to the shore. Beyond the horizon of the sea which crashed on the beach before me the nearest land lay thousands of miles away – the east coast of Africa. In Perth one really did feel on the edge of the world if you looked West. In the water dozens of surfers, dressed in multi-coloured, fluorescent shorts and T shirts did their amazing tricks, curling and gliding, weaving and turning, whilst I was the only one in the water trying to swim. The odd Englishman in navy blue trunks staring at the sea.

I was sorry to leave. In just over two weeks I had become acclimatised to this strange planet. Other people's kitchens no longer held any fear for me; I had developed an instinctive skill for finding out where people kept tea-bags, muesli, bath plugs, ironing boards, alarm clocks and bread. I felt at home, known; people began to ring me up on the phone. And it was all gone twenty-four hours later, on the other side of the world, wiping a strange sand from my shoes, looking out into our garden at the leaves turning brown on the trees and remembering the day before, when I'd watched green parakeets searching the dunes for twigs to build nests. It was like being in one of those sealed glass bottles: turn it one way and snowflakes tumble down on your head, turn it the other way and you stand in a clear light.

11 Perth – Hobart – Sydney – Darwin – Alice Springs May 1992

I'm back in the familiar attic, facing a blank screen. It's 5.30 am, May bank holiday weekend, my body has not yet fully adjusted to its new reverse timetable – day is night, night is day – but it is a beautiful morning, the sky through the dormer window is powder blue, and the garden below in other times I would have referred to as being as profuse and luxuriant as a tropical jungle. But two weeks ago I was sitting in the middle of a tropical jungle at the opening night of the Darwin Literary Festival, with frogs jumping out of the trees and into the beer glasses, and it is rather different. Let's just say that the garden, immediately out there, now, with the lilac coming into bloom, the horse chestnut flowers starting to appear, the apple blossom, the elderflowers and the bluebells, and the dozen varieties of green, is reassuring. And see, I've started to set it all down.

I was asked out by the Institute for Cultural Policy Studies at Griffith University in Brisbane, to speak on questions of urban and cultural policy. In turn they contacted all the seven Australian State Ministries – Western Australia, South Australia, Victoria, New South Wales, Tasmania, Queensland, Northern Territories – offering my services as a lecturer while I was out there. All of them responded, and so I got to fly to a dozen different towns and cities throughout Australia, some as far apart as London is from Moscow or North Africa, and one of them so remote, Albany, an ex-whaling town in the far south-west, I flew there in a 12 seater, piloted by an amiable old boy who looked as though when he wasn't flying his little Cessna he was farming pigs. (A notice stuck on to the refreshment kiosk door at Albany Airport, no bigger than a minicab office, said: 'Pilots Please Note. The keys to the reception desk should not be left on the premises, if you are the last to leave.')

In all I gave 28 lectures, conducted 19 seminars, and did nine radio and three television interviews. The arrangements went like clockwork: all I had to do was get up in the morning (usually at some unearthly hour), pack, take a taxi to the airport, catch the plane itemised on my itinerary, be met at the other end by someone whom I would always recognise as they would me by intuition, get taken to another hotel and told where to turn up next. I was passed from one city to the next like a parcel, affectionately and kindly. A strange way of life.

The strangeness of it all was compounded by the world of hotel rooms: part monastic cells, part gold-tapped and flouncy curtained bordello suites, a Gideon Bible in one drawer and a catalogue of adult videos for hire in the other. No one to talk to, but bottles of champagne in the *en suite* bar. In fact, ideal places for writing letters and postcards, and reflecting on life. Reflecting on others things too. One of the most disorientating aspects of staying in hotels is that the mirrors are in different places from the ones you are used to at home, and you are frequently unnerved to catch a sight of yourself from a wholly new angle. Who is this stranger in my room? My friend Stephen once assured me that within the Quaker tradition, mirrors were not allowed in the house, presumably because of the temptations to vanity and self-love.

I moved on about every four days, for a month, a portable life complete with novels, writing pads, document files, a tiny cassette radio/player and half a dozen tapes, a guide to Australian birds, a Swiss army pen-knife, a hole puncher and small staple gun. I realised that the more you travelled alone the more your own sense of self began to diminish and attenuate. The sheer impact of the external world, the constant and insistent strangeness and newness of things, made the inner life almost non-existent for a while. This is certainly not unpleasant. There's a freedom in mobility, a certain lightness of being.

After a month Larraine flew out to join me, and we stayed for most of the time in Sydney and Brisbane, though occasionally I flew off for a couple of days to another part of the what seemed like the globe. There were a lot of in-flight snacks and a lot of cellophane to undo to get at them. Sixteen separate flights in all. I would happily do it again. For I love Australia – its climate, its intellectual openness, the balance between physical enjoyment and the life of the mind, the quality of the light, its lack of snobbery, and so on. Of course there are deep problems – of history, of the insoluble dilemma of the aboriginal peoples, a lost tribe wandering literally through the deserts of the cities 30,000 years out of time, of political corruption – but as a visitor, now for the second time, I'm mostly captivated by it all. Dense, urban, European baroque intensity is no longer the unqualified good I thought it once was.

Certainly it was a good place to be for a British general election, which rarely got more coverage in the Australian press than a supermarket robbery in Woollongong or Parramatta, and from which distance the issues being debated in Britain seemed telescopically small. And by the way, I'm afraid I never for a moment doubted that the Conservatives would win. I'm sorry, but white, mortgaged, middle England is terrified of change, of the foreignness of Europe, of unemployed Northerners or people with funny Welsh or Scottish proletarian accents. Middle England will cleave to the Conservative Party for dear life. Whenever I leave Britain now, on the occasions when I travel abroad, I feel like I'm walking out of the doors of a museum that is shortly to close.

This time I went to Australia partly in the spirit of two earlier English sensibilities: D.H. Lawrence and Bruce Chatwin. I took both *Kangaroo* and *The Songlines* with me, and I read them *in situ.* One weekend we spent near Mullumbimby on the coast of New South Wales, where Lawrence and Frieda briefly settled, and we looked out through the Norfolk Island pines on to the same beaches and the wild Pacific Ocean that he did. In Alice Springs, late one night, I went for a walk through the deserted town, and found an Italian cafe where the night people go, and I knew that Chatwin had been there. I also talked to the woman in the bookshop and gallery that he described in the opening pages of *The Songlines,* the very same woman, and, unusually for me, I wanted to be in touch with the characters in that inspiring book.

In Darwin and Alice Springs I felt the palpable 'otherness' of some parts of Australia, its sheer age and mystery, its arid bleakness and terror (to these constrained, flat Essex and North London eyes) completely cutting across and undermining the apparent modern society now built there. Not so much 'beneath the paving stones, the beach', but beyond the city limits the relatively brief era of human development has yet to begin. Out there, there is geological time only, rocks, stones, desert, primeval swampland, incomprehensible distances, a landscape obdurately resistant to human life, and even 'nature' itself. Beyond nature in fact. Flying over the Simpson Desert, among several deserts I crossed on the trip, even at 35,000 feet the cloudless skies enable one to observe the endless barrenness of it all in apparent microscopic detail, parched rock or sand, occasional small mountain ranges, or a few million square miles of dunes, more lunar than the moon itself.

In the process of moving every few days to a completely new city, I had confirmed what I'd always assumed, that people are passionately keen to describe to strangers the uniqueness of the place in which they live. I would say that this is as powerful as self-confession, a form of topophilia, if there is such a condition. At times this had its dangers, as when in the course of the car ride from the airport to the city centre, my new hosts would point out every topographical or historical feature on the way, sometimes taking both hands off the wheel and completely averting their eyes from the freeway to demonstrate to me how, for example, the forest fires which raged in 1988 on the western side of Mount Wellington nearly wiped out a whole suburb, over there, see just to the left of the giant radio pylon, and so on. I was often more intent on wondering whether my guide/driver had noticed the 16 wheel, 24 headlight, timber truck bearing down on us as we wandered into its path while engaged in our visual diversion. Safer in the plane.

This was always happening. Enthusiastic people, delighted to be able to be the first to interpret their city to a stranger, narrowly avoided mowing down gangs of road-menders, drove through red traffic lights, just about avoided being crushed between two airport buses as they came off the slip road on to the freeway at exactly the same moment that they noticed a small outcrop of ironstone which was an aboriginal sacred site, and in a dozen other ways put my heart in my mouth as I struggled between the pleasures of topography and the instinct for survival that made me want to grab the steering wheel and bring us back on to the right side of the road.

In Hobart I was told the tragic story of the bridge disaster at least six times, and every person who told me had fashioned their version of the events as they had remembered them. Hobart is built, like many towns and cities, on both sides of a river estuary, now connected by a modern bridge. In 1975, early one evening, a cargo ship hit one of the pillars of the Tasman Bridge, bringing down a section with a number of cars on it, and also sinking the ship and her crew. Some dozens of lives were lost. In a small isolated city, this had all the ingredients of a great historic tragedy, which it was. I was variously told additional human interest stories to embellish the bald facts – of the car which had stopped with the two front wheels overhanging the broken bridge, of the driver who had gone to help and had fallen to his death, of the doctor driving home after having just visiting his wife and their new baby in hospital, whose body was not found for three months, and even of people who, it was darkly hinted, had used the opportunity to leave Hobart for quite different reasons altogether. Yet the biggest impact of this disaster was on the social structure of Hobart, for with the bridge gone it was a 60 kilometres drive from the north shore to the city centre, just two kilometres as the crow flies across the water. It took several years to build a new bridge, during which close knit families or friends who visited each other sometimes daily, hardly ever met socially again. Few new buildings were put up in the north shore and the two parts of a single city drifted apart and developed wholly new social relations and separate identities.

Vignette: Tidying up the slides and slide projector after my public lecture at the Hobart Museum and Gallery, one of the staff gestured over to a corner of the giant Custom House building in which we were standing to a large collection of boxes covered in dust sheets. 'You'll never guess what that lot is. It's Clive Jenkins' personal collection of British trade union memorabilia. He wants to sell it to us but we don't have the money to buy it.'

In order to relax and get some exercise away from the rather enervating life of seminars, lectures, restaurants and bars, I went swimming as often as I could. When I got to a new hotel the first question was: where's the nearest swimming pool? I swam, like Burt Lancaster in *The Swimmer*, in chronological and topographical order, in the Esplanade Hotel pool, Fremantle; the Indian Ocean, Fremantle; the Adelaide Olympic Pool; the City Baths, Melbourne; the Hobart Olympic Pool; Toowong Public Swimming Pool, Brisbane; the Pacific Ocean, Queensland; a private pool in Indooropilly, Brisbane; Sydney Olympic Pool; the Andrew 'Boy' Charlton Pool in Sydney; Manley Beach; Bondi Beach; Byron Beach, NSW; the Darwin Hotel pool; and in a private pool on the Sunshine Coast at Marcus Beach. By my third visit to an Australian pool I noticed that I was the only one doing the breast-stroke. Arriving, finally, at base in Brisbane, I asked my friend, Colin, with whom I was staying, with why this was so, and being a sociologist he told me thus: 'You should understand, Ken, that in Australia, swimming strokes are deeply gendered.' In short I wasn't a real man.

In some pools the lanes were even divided into Freestyle Only and Breast-Stroke Only and guess who was usually the only man in the latter? Checking in at the Russell Hotel in Sydney at Circular Quay, I asked the receptionist, 'Where's the nearest pool?' She had a couple of friends hanging round the desk chatting, so they conferred. 'I guess the pool over in the Domain is nearest,' one said. 'Oh, I don't think the gentleman would like that,' the receptionist said, rather worriedly, 'it's rather, how shall we say, local.' 'What do you mean, local?' 'Well it's used a lot by the gays. It's a bit of a hangout.' The pool turned out to be the appropriately named Andrew 'Boy' Charlton pool, usually just called 'the Boy'.

My favourite pools were the open-air pool in Hobart, with a fine view of Mount Wellington (just the place to escape and completely envelop oneself in the watery element), the Olympic pool in Sydney, built for the nineteen twenty something Olympics, immediately below the Sydney Harbour Bridge so you look up into this giant meccano set, finely surrounded by art deco glass and mosaic perimeter walls; and the Toowong pool in Brisbane, a small municipal pool with never more than a dozen people and to which I always went when there was time and the temperature got into the upper 20s.

Swimming baths fascinate me, their arcane rules and regulations, their gloomy basements, the chlorine and urine-smelling changing rooms, and occasionally – in Australia – the dazzling heat and light in and by the pool. The municipal pool needs its own Foucault. They remain unique when every other kind of public or commercial institution has become the same. In the existential search for authenticity, for the gluey, viscous, rank facticity of things, you can't beat a good old-fashioned municipal pool.

I tried body surfing one day, but Larraine said all she ever saw were my legs in the air upside down. I got 'dumped' several times by giant waves and learned to be careful. The Pacific coast is where the real surfers go, and although it's fun to be in among the waves, it's impossible to swim. The fun is riding the waves and occasionally swimming in on the crest of a breaking wave and being carried along, almost flying, by its massive power. Every so often, though, a real monster suddenly appears, a ten feet high sheer wall of blue-green water, capable of pounding concrete into powder. This is known as a dumper. All you can do is face it and dive into it as low as possible, as if through a plate glass window like James Bond. Mostly it works; when it doesn't you are picked up, spun around helplessly for a couple of seconds in a whirling maelstrom, water and sand buffeting your face and roaring in your ears, and then hurtled onto the hard sand with the force of being thrown from a ten-storey window. It hurts.

The real surfers I now realise actually come from another planet. If you look at them closely enough you'll see that they aren't really human. They haven't developed the facial muscles that allow them to smile, although they have over-developed muscles everywhere else. Larraine pointed out to me that they also walk quite differently to human beings; a web-footed kind of walk as if they have suction pads on their feet. I think they are occasionally brought in by the sea at night and left on the beach to crawl their way into human society, unbeknown. One dusk we drove to the Lennox Heads, a spectacular headland in New South Wales, a few miles from the paradisal Byron Bay. It was getting dark, and the water had a wild, grey, gloomy gothic look to it. A mile from where we stood we could see these tiny feral sea creatures drifting out to sea in the half-light, each very alone, doubtlessly cold and hungry but obsessed, and then catching a wave, standing upright and hurtling in perhaps a half mile in less than a minute, weaving and threading their way through the waves, only to finally sink beneath the water and start crawling out again into the terminally darkening sea. It is a monotheistic religion; it demands excessive sacrifice and self-denial; it's a penance, perhaps, for living in such a lovely country.

This time I learned a rather obvious fact that had eluded me on my previous visit, and in most of the things I'd read about Australia: all the indigenous mammals are nocturnal. None of them are hard-footed either. This is very important because it has been realised that the wholesale introduction of sheep and cattle in the nineteenth century has worn down the thin topsoil in many states to nothing. People are now arguing for the cultivation and farming of kangaroos for meat and by-products, the natural soft-padded inhabitant of the land, if any grazing country is to be left at all. The introduction of, variously, the rabbit, the cat, the fox, the starling, the convolvulus, dandelions and cultivated grass, among many other introduced flora and fauna has had catastrophic effects. The cats went wild and today account for massive species-decimation among parrots and other indigenous birds. Rabbits stripped whole plains and regions of the natural vegetation. Cattle and sheep ground the topsoil into arid dust. There's a 5,765 kilometre Dingo Fence which runs across the width of Australia to prevent the dingoes from getting into the lusher grazing lands of the East. Western Australia prides itself on having successfully kept the sparrow out of the territory; those that manage to cross the central deserts are 'shot at the border' I was told. But in the long-term the situation is very bleak. As Alfred Crosby notes in his magisterial study, *Biological Imperialism*, eventually, 'the dandelion will triumph over the kangaroo'.

Awareness of these ecological issues is widely shared; many conversations at some point talk about before and after certain animals or plants were 'introduced'; there's a popular culture around questions of indigenous flora and fauna; everybody seems to know their 138 varieties of the gum tree or the courtship habits of the bower bird. I did get a chance to see a bower bird nest, in a part of the rainforest in the Blue Mountains. The male bower bird builds an elaborate tent or shelter on the ground by bending twigs over and weaving them. Then he fills it with blue objects – biro tops, bits of blue detergent bottle, blue glass, copies of Conservative Party election manifestos, Melbourne bus tickets – and then waits around for a prospective female to entice into this elegant palisade. Wonderful. In the same setting, great currawongs and crimson rosellas perched in the trees just feet from one's head: the former a raven-size black and white bird with chilling yellow eyes, the latter a large blue and red parrot of breathtaking beauty. The Blue Mountains are called so because the density of the eucalyptus forests emits a bluish evaporation into the air; looking down into a heavily wooded valley there is a blue haze; actually not unlike a bluebell wood. In all the history of biological transmigration between Europe and the 'new worlds' of Australia and North and South America, Crosby noted, only one plant (and no animals) successfully reversed the tide of ecological imperialism outwards, and that is the eucalyptus tree, which is now found in great profusion in Spain and some other Mediterranean countries. And in our own garden, too. We have a stunning tree, with silvery-green leaves which glitter in the wind, and with pearly white fronds at the top as delicate as fennel.

Every city is quite different from the others: as different as

European capitals are from each other in fact. Elegant, Victorian and Edwardian Adelaide, is entirely free of the convict past: it was freely settled and lets everybody know it. Melbourne is a tram-dominated, dark stone built Mitteleuropa, a cosmopolitan city with gothic, punk and avant-garde subcultures. Sydney is as brash as New York, an astonishingly beautiful harbour, a gloomy, dirty skyscraper-dominated central business district, and a gay quarter of such vitality, colour and exuberance, that once you've found it it's the only place to be. Taxis are cheap and plentiful everywhere, the drivers are friendly, the only problem is that they usually haven't a clue as to where they are going. Most of them seem to have arrived in the city even more recently than you have. In Brisbane I regularly got a cab from where I was staying in the suburbs to the West End district, where the academics and the hippies live: to visit friends, to give talks. Pick up a phone and the taxi is usually there before you've opened the front door.

G'day mate. (Yes, they really do say it.) And how are you today?

Fine, thanks. West End, please.

Sure. No worries, mate.

The cab starts off in the wrong direction.

Actually I think the best route is over the Indooropilly Bridge.

Sure, mate. No worries. Where in the West End?

Edmondstone Street. You know it?

Don't think so, mate. Actually I don't know Brisbane very well. I'm from Sydney. I'll look it up.

Most taxi rides end up with the driver spreading out the large format street map over the steering wheel and reading his way while driving.

Whoops, sorry about that mate.

In the end my nerves wouldn't allow me to ride in cabs in which the drivers pored over the street index while negotiating round-abouts and freeways with one corner of an eye and just a little finger on the wheel. I made them look it up before we set off. This caused no offence at all. If you were a couple of dollars short of the fare in change, and only had a 50 dollar note the driver would see your predicament and accept the lower sum. No worries, mate. That's fine. They really didn't worry overmuch about anything; and that attitude, that in the end everything can be sorted out, is what endeared me to the country. Although I did tire of everybody asking me how I was today – the newsagent, the bus driver, the ticket clerk, the young woman in the chemists when I went to stock up with codeine for a terrible bout of flu I developed immediately on arriving in Australia – I grew more and more envious of the easy familiarity and helpfulness that characterised most public transactions between strangers. Catch up with you later, said the Customs official at Perth after he'd stamped my passport when I arrived and waved me on. See you again, soon, mate, said the taxi-driver taking me to Alice Springs airport, as if he ever would.

Some of it's rote; some of it's genuine. Whenever we went out to eat in restaurants the people we were with always treated the waiters or waitresses as intellectual equals – there was no hierarchy in the relationship at all: there would be a bit of chat about things, advice of what to eat, the waiter would be offered a glass of wine, and occasionally in the more radical places might even be invited to sit down for a while to have a chat and a drink if they weren't immediately busy. Often this was because they were friends or acquaintances, earning extra money to support a college place or a young family.

Some of the hospitality ethos is clearly American in origin, and there's still a lot of American influence about although it's fading rapidly as the whole country is turning to face and become part of the Pacific rim. The Anglo-Saxon sun is setting; the White Australia Policy of the Cold War years and earlier is now gone. Only the die-hards believe that Australia's future is still tied to Queen and Mother Parliament. Geography is destiny; the great paradox that hits you when you first visit Australia and find a suburban English culture set down in the middle of a sub-tropical continent, will over time be resolved. Australia is now a multicultural country, with an increasing Asian inflection to much of its street life and culture. Vietnamese immigration now out-numbers British immigration I was told. But some American attitudes and influences are still quite strong, a hangover from the days when American culture replaced British culture in people's demotic and democratic aspirations.

At the Darwin poetry evening, to which I'd gone on my own, a stranger in town, sipping beers as the fruit bats whizzed over my head and the sweat poured from my face (and the frogs dropped into the beer glasses from the giant palms overhead), I got talking to some of the people at my table. In fact they introduced themselves. Hi, I'm Troy, this is Carol and Annie and you are? Ken. Hi, Ken. Hi, Troy. Hi Carol, Hi Annie. What do you do Troy? I'm in hospitality. Hospitality turned out to be working in a friend's run down cafe in a run down shopping mall. But again Troy exemplified the open spirit of the place. I suspect he'd done a lot of drugs in earlier years – and he was still just a bit punch-drunk. But soon he'd go out on the trawlers, he said, just move on for a while; get a change of scene and find out a bit more about himself.

Troy was not one of them but Darwin has a very large population of transient people; people who've come to the end of their existential journey. It's strange and slightly scary. I guess that in Britain people who come to the end of their tether, and go mad or hit the streets and the bottle still mostly stay around were they live; in Australia losers move to Darwin. In addition to an aboriginal population of several thousand who live in the streets, there are several thousand white people living rough. They are mostly men, in shorts and thongs, sitting in the parks, sleeping in the bush, drinking, and slightly crazed by the sun and the humidity. I realised in Darwin where all that *Mad Max* iconography comes from. Some have enough money to hang out in the pubs, or visit the prostitutes. Darwin is a twentieth century equivalent of the Wild West. 'Prawn and porn', is how the one acquaintance described the dominant culture of Darwin, as we drove down a strip of bars and clubs with blackened windows advertising strippers, baked-bean wrestling and happy hour.

Troy and I got on but disagreed about the poetry. The first poet who read was among the worst I have ever listened to. High on cheap wine, he ran on stage (the deck of an old sailing-ship moored inland and serving as a bar/restaurant), beat his breast and shouted to us that he was angry. Yes angry. He raved, and ranted, told us how much he suffered for his art, described to us his dreams and nightmares (which were indistinguishable) and read strings of words of the utmost banality. It was the old, 'I've suffered for my art and now it's your turn.' Amazing, man, said Troy shaking his head. I think I'm a bit too old for that kind of thing, I compromised. This poseur actually read a completely meaningless poem which he subsequently told us was made up of all the last words of all his old poems. Clever stuff, eh? Then he finished with 'a poem I wrote last night', words which always signal the death of literature. For what this ominous phrase means, decoded, is: automatic writing, spontaneity, night-time angst, no re-writing, emotion unmediated by thought, no element of editing or endless re-formulation involved. Crap at the start and crap at the finish. I went to fetch another round of drinks.

But there was some lovely stuff subsequently, witty, poignant, heart-breaking; when good poetry is read well, the experience is hard to beat. I finished the evening in a haze of goodwill and high emotion. The walk home (I noticed I always referred to returning to my hotel as getting 'back home') in the oppressive night air, with Troy escorting me half way back into town, but with a late night bar at the hotel to stop and have just one more ice cold beer before bed, was quite memorable.

Time and place. Much of Australia's difficult and almost hopeless past history is tied up in the names of places, which are Aboriginal, early settler or straightforward colonial. Many towns and place do preserve the aboriginal names, though given a more orthodox spelling: Wagga Wagga, Indooropilly, Paramatta, Woollongong. But to my eyes and ears it is the names chosen by the first convict settlers which provide the deepest resonance: Broken Hill, Hopeless Creek, Fog Bay, Doubtful Island Bay, Cape Catastrophe, Deaf Adder Creek, Tin Can Creek, Saddle Hill. Subsequent naming was colonial and unimaginative to a degree: in Newcastle, NSW, I was driven around the local suburbs which were called, respectively, Stockport, Glasgow, Jesmond, Cardiff, Wallsend, Islington, Swansea and Toronto – all within a radius of 15 miles. In Sydney Larraine and I took a suburban train out to Liverpool one evening, passing through Dulwich, Eastbourne, Sydenham and other spectral arcadias summoned up from 10,000 miles away, but now in fact pre-dominantly Vietnamese or Italian. Every Australian city has a Paddington, a Kings Cross, a Macquarie Street, a Leichhardt Street, a Bourke Street and a Collins Street – these last four being the names of the early explorers. But it's hardly imaginative to have all your cities sharing almost the same street directory of place names.

The last engagement, the terminal point as it were in the whole trip, was in Alice Springs. A place one can never forget. Alice Springs is certainly best reached by air. People have died trying to make it by road, though most still do by bus, coach or lorry. There's also a train, twice weekly, along a single track from Adelaide, probably about 1200 miles with no stops across a barren rocky desert. Flying in, one is suddenly confronted by a set of almost perfectly formed high ridges – the Macdonnell Ranges – which run parallel for about 350 miles. In a tiny space between the two ridges is an almost perfectly formed Basildon. The nearest town is probably at least 500 miles in any direction. You could be on the moon. The weather is arid and hot all year round with one tropical storm once a year. Through the centre of this quite ugly town, runs a wide river bed, the Todd River, again which floods once a year but for the rest of the year is dry and sandy, though filled with quite large red gums and ghost gums. In this river bed hundreds of aboriginals live, squatting round camp fires, sleeping in the open, rigging up bits of old cloth or sacking to create some shade.

There is apparently no planning legislation, and my host, a geographical photographer, drove me round to a series of hideous motels, private housing developments, all built without any reference to the topography or climate of the place – Hawaiian beach villages for tourists, suburban houses with green lawns that soak up more water per day than is piped to aboriginal out-stations in a year, great disfiguring public housing estates built on land requiring traditional aboriginal sacred sites to be cleared and levelled. Alice Springs has a civic culture in the way Siberia has a cafe society. They recently built a new shopping centre which killed off the rest of the town's shops and then itself ran into trouble and closed. The town is filled with tourist shops selling facsimile aboriginal art – dot shops, the local cynics call them, after the dot-painting style of the Arrente aboriginals which has become a kind of generic tradition – though they are all run by white people and one suspects that if an aboriginal dared step foot inside them the police would be called immediately. The whole town felt like living in a greyhound bus that had broken down in an unmapped continent. And walking round, late one night, the heat produced a kind of eerie silence in the deserted streets, although occasionally one could see at a distance small groups of aboriginals huddled together in the trees, or on a park bench, or stretched out in an empty shopping mall. There was absolutely no interaction between the white and the aboriginals at all, as far as I could see, no eye contact, no exchanges of greetings, nothing.

I was given a handbook which explained the totemic geography of the place, as far as the indigenous aboriginals understood their landscape. Every hill, ridge, rock outcrop, hillock had its place in a complicated myth connected with the caterpillar ancestors of the Alice Springs aboriginals. Some rocks were lost children, others bits of dogs eaten by caterpillars, many were caterpillars themselves, or kangaroos. As Chatwin describes in *The Songlines*, every inch of the landscape is part of a continuous narrative that continues to this day. But the insensitivity and the greed of local developers knows no bounds. The good burghers of Alice Springs decided they needed a casino. The site was adjacent to one of the great caterpillar rocks. One Bank Holiday afternoon, Christmas 1983 in fact, there was a large bang and people walked out to find the tail of the caterpillar had been dynamited to make room for a lorry entrance to the site. Broken Promise Drive the aboriginals call this road; and the sullenness deepens. Local activists sought prosecution of the developers under the Sacred Sites Act, which was thrown out of court as it transpired that the Act was not binding on land owned by the crown. (That's our fragrant queen, great white mother many thousands of miles away.) In the aboriginal section of the State Art Gallery for the Northern Territories, several of the art works had sections blanked out with paper glued on to the glass bearing the hand-written notice: 'Please do not remove. Sacred items taped. Thank you. Tandanya.'

You will gather that I love Australia. And yes I could live there, but I won't. Larraine doesn't feel quite as enthusiastic as I do, but she certainly liked it. I also was made to realise the costs of such a transformation in one's life, when on the very first Sunday I was there, in Fremantle, the woman who was acting as my host invited me to breakfast on the beach (I was due to fly out in the afternoon) to meet a good friend of theirs whom I probably knew of: the Geordie folk-singer Alex Glasgow, now settled in Perth. In fact not only did I know of him, but I'd had dealings with him over a Blair Peach benefit I helped organise at the Royal Court and at which he performed. He's a lovely man, then and now. But he'd given it all up; completely wiped the first 50 years of his life clean. He no longer wrote, and no longer sang, I was told. He swam every day, cycled every day, kept an allotment and did the housework while his wife, a social worker, went out to work. He looked slim, tanned and very fit but I did not envy him. It's tempting, of course, to start again. Like one or two of those people in Hobart who took advantage of the collapse of the bridge and the drownings to walk off into the night, take a ferry or a plane, change their names and start all over again. Two lives for the price of one: it's tempting. I also think it would be unbearable. It would be like one of those *grand guignol* films in which the murderer who has buried the body still keeps dreaming about it, can never quite get rid of all the evidence, and years after the body floats to the surface of the lake or is dug up by a contractor's digger, and the investigation starts all over again. I don't think I could bury my past like that: my body wouldn't fit into the boot of the car; Epping Forest wouldn't be big enough.

Other travels now beckon. In fact I've just returned from an overnight trip to Bolton, a trip more fraught with disasters and cultural dissonances in its way than Australia. In Australia I travelled at least 6,000 miles within the country, and was never late once. My afternoon train to Bolton was already an hour behind schedule 30 miles out of London: points failure at Bletchley. The person I was to meet in the evening for a social drink – before a potentially difficult meeting on Monday – had given up by the time I'd got to Bolton, tired and frazzled. It was a quarter to ten on a Sunday evening and Bolton town centre was very quiet indeed. I walked up the road to one of Bolton's more classy restaurants, an art-deco pizzeria, just in time to get a *pizza al fungi* and a small carafe of red wine before it closed. I was only there for half an hour but I had to sing 'Happy Birthday' twice. Then I remembered, Boltonians only eat out like this on people's birthdays. So every 15 minutes a cracked tape, like a pilot's announcement, comes over the PA system playing 'Happy Birthday' and everybody in the restaurant is supposed to sing.

The suntans in Bolton were brighter than anything I'd seen in Australia. Actually I wasn't unhappy being on the move again. Returning to London the next day, the connecting train from Bolton to Manchester was late, just missing the Manchester train by five minutes. I waited an hour for the next train which itself was running 18 minutes late by the time we reached London. Anger is a wasted emotion. I'm learning to come to terms with the fact that Britain is different. It is a museum; the attendants are rather sleepy; the exhibits are gathering dust. But every so often you have to step outside, for a bit of fresh air, for a glimpse of the sun.

12 Belfast – Omagh March 1993

Apart from the roadblocks in the middle of the larger towns, from which camouflaged and blacked-up soldiers train machine guns on you and your car from behind mounds of sandbags and barbed wire, while an amiable, London-accented West Indian soldier stops then waves you on wishing you a safe journey, the roads in rural Northern Ireland are delightful. This is what Raymond Williams called a 'working landscape': hill farms, new bungalows, tractors on the road everywhere, petrol stations now substituting for shops, the smell of silage and cattle feed, chimney smoke, and layers of rain clouds dashing themselves against the hills. The fields and copses are full of rooks and jackdaws, more than I've ever seen in such concentrations before. This is my second visit in the last six months and it is, as always, raining. But gusty rain, patches of sun, four seasons in a day type weather. I've been doing some work on the future of public libraries, and there is considerable interest in the project in Northern Ireland, particularly in Belfast and Omagh. This visit is to talk to the staff and begin to build up a picture of public library use in the province, but of course for me it's more than that: it is movement, strangeness, newness, something to slough off the general lassitude of British politics and daily life.

I hired a car at Belfast airport and drove straight to Omagh in the late afternoon, the longer way round Lough Neagh, avoiding the motorway route which would be quicker and simpler but only in the sense that death is quicker and simpler. Omagh is an attractive county town in County Tyrone, but it is heavily sandbagged and fortressed. The hotel I stay at, a business motel, is almost next door to the RUC headquarters, which looks like a giant retail shed without the doors. It is all corrugated tin cladding, giant metal fencing, barbed wire and security cameras. Every building above four storeys and every surrounding hilltop sports a red-lighted antenna, presumably to guide the helicopters which pass overhead every hour or so at no more than 80 feet, through the labyrinth of the rooftops. I managed to find a pub that sold food in the town centre, had something to eat and walked around for a while, until 9 o'clock when the town centre was barricaded and closed to traffic by RUC officers and army soldiers, all carrying machine guns. The only people on the streets were some friendly 12 year old kids hanging round one of the pub doors. In Logan's Bar, where I had a pint of Guinness before going back to the hotel, the men sitting at the bar watching the television were visibly upset as the James Bulger story unfolded on the screen – the body had just been found. The barman was very friendly, and conversational but often I found it difficult to understand what he was saying, so thick and ululating was his accent. But I love the accent, which has a rich, slightly querulous, questioning and sing song rhythm to it; but filtered through gravel. In women's speech it is even more enchanting.

Back at the hotel it is obvious there is a function going on; I shall know more about this later. In bed by 10.30 after *News at Ten*, I'm asleep in seconds. Then the fire alarm goes. I sit up panicking. It's 2.30 in the morning and the fire bell is ringing – and then stopping – ringing and then stopping. Out of bed I find my glasses and read the notice on the door: The Fire Alarm Sounds a Continuous Ring. Guests should make their way to the car park immediately. But nobody else along this ground floor corridor is moving. Everything goes quiet. At 3 and 3.15 it rings again, and then someone bangs on the window. I'm out in the corridor in no time in an overcoat and shoes, into the main hall only to find large numbers of young people in evening dress, very drunk, mostly in couples, draped at the bottom of the stairs or in the bar, either swearing undying love or being violently sick. Another guest sees my confusion and assures me it was just a false alarm – bloody kids. The following morning, after breakfast which is eaten in silence alongside several tables full of salesmen and travellers in cattle food who invariably get up from the table saying 'Let battle commence', I get the picture.

It was a 'formal'. One of the librarians explains when I tell my story: just the local grammar school sixth-form having an annual dinner and dance (and collapse and vomit). There was one almost every other night at the hotel. Just last week 'your man Paisley' was the guest speaker at a local Unionist 'formal', and an organ had been set up at the high table for hymns before and after the food. It is, I suppose, characteristic of rural areas to develop this kind of formal associational culture. 'We have to belong...' another librarian tells me as I dig deeper. So there are all kinds of organisations to belong to – religious, political, masonic, young farmers, college, hobbies – all with a regular calendar of dinner and dances, speeches, presentations, shields and cups, ladies nights, long-serving medals, and all providing occasions for a chance to dress up and have a night out.

The next night I'm in a slightly different state of shock. It has been arranged for me to stay in a 'very respectable' guest house some 20 miles from Belfast, to which one of my hosts will drive me in the evening, and also arrange for me to join him for a meal. But in Omagh no message comes from Belfast about arrangements at all, despite endless phone calls: your man has gone missing. In fact back in Belfast dialling from a call box to the fourth number on a scribbled list I find out that due to sudden illness the arrangements have been cancelled. I'm given the name and address of the guest house which is an expensive taxi-ride out into the middle of nowhere: a hamlet in total darkness on the road to Lorne. When I get there I'm tired and slightly resentful: I could have spent the night staying in the city and had a look round. Worse follows. No, they don't do evening meals and they're temperance. But, they tell me, about a mile down the road is a country club.

The room is very respectable: screamingly so. Wallpaper, curtains, bedcovers and carpet compete in clashing floral patterns, scallops and frills, like one of those childhood nightmares when you had a fever and all the colours ran inside your head like liquid marble. And above the bed is a framed text:

> Sleep sweet within this quiet room
> For thou so weary art!
> And let no mournful yesterdays
> Disturb thy peaceful heart
>
> Nor let tomorrow mar thy rest
> With dreams of coming ill
> Thy MAKER is thy changeless FRIEND
> His love surrounds thee still;
>
> Forget thyself and all the world,
> Put out each little light
> The stars are watching overhead,
> Sleep sweet – Good night, Good night.

Out in the dark I scramble along a grassy kerb, my path lit only by the occasional pair of headlights. The country club looks like something out of one of those American '50s 'B' movies: security gates, a uniformed porter in a small gate-house opening the gates for the cars and distinctly suspicious of someone walking in from the open road. There is a large campus of motel chalets, fitness suites, stables, and two main buildings. Inside one of them it is vaulted, timbered and very expensive. There is a gauntlet of waiters and waitresses to run through just to get to the bar. As I arrive the bar is emptying to the sound of a single bag-piper who begins leading a phalanx of men in suits towards the baronial dining room, leaving me virtually on my own. This is the pattern for the evening. I go into the public restaurant to find seven staff looking at me and then rushing towards me. I have two wine waiters and five food waiters dancing attendance on me, as the only person in the elegant dining room. I read the menu from right to left: price first, item second. In fact they know that I know that they know that I'm a bit out of my depth. The halibut in oyster and champagne sauce is actually quite nice, and by far the cheapest dish; the Australian wine is one I drank last year on a beach, but then at a quarter of the cost. In the end the good people of Belfast are paying for this but I'd rather they didn't.

Let me say that I have never felt anything less than completely safe in Northern Ireland. The centre of Belfast is just another busy shopping city; the people are very friendly, and there's something quite tenacious, open-hearted and stoic about the place. It must be the need to live in a city constantly chilled by the winds off the lough, and the rain from the sea. There is nothing genteel about it; it's a tough city like Liverpool or Glasgow. And it has fine eighteenth and nineteenth century buildings and institutions, the finest of which is the Linen Hall Library. This is one of the few remaining subscription libraries anywhere in Britain or Ireland, located in Donegall Square. A handsome doorway leads directly (though past a porter) to a wide flight of stairs leading up to the library; as you get to the top of the stairs you are suddenly back in the nineteenth century, a book-lined vast study area, with window seats, piles of old newspapers on the floor, someone serving coffee, a dusty clutter of books and people absorbed and moderated by reading and quiet conversation. This is truly a magical place; it feels wholly lived in and loved – and quite unacademic and unpretentious. There is a good description of it in one of Seamus Heaney's essays:

> Apart from its great and irreplaceable collection and its enhancing contribution to the cultural and intellectual life of generations, the 'Linen Hall' is one of those living proofs that the golden age of the city had not been lived in vain; the moral and imaginative quickening that took place in the late eighteenth century always revives for me when I go up those stairs.

The poet Tom Paulin has also written a fine tribute to it. We need to re-invigorate public libraries as centres for lectures, pamphlets and debates, although I am still surprised at how popular and well used public libraries are. In Northern Ireland they are the only neutral, non-sectarian spaces left, where politics and religion are still left at the door.

* * *

Yesterday was Purim. The streets in this part of Stoke Newington were mayhem. Purim is a Jewish festival, a version of the medieval Festival of Fools. My mother, who lives round the corner, noticed it when she went to put out her rubbish and saw two middle-aged matrons standing on the corner gossiping with balloons tied to their hair. All day long cars circled the streets blaring their horns, covered in balloons and tinsel. Children wandered around the streets dressed as clowns, as spoof rabbis, as Mickey Mouses, a lot of them with loud-hailers singing songs and telling jokes against the adults. 12 year olds lit cigarettes in front of their parents and blew smoke in their faces. An open top double decker bus drove up and down our road with about 40 young men in black Homburgs and crombie coats dancing to taped music. It is wholly wonderful because it seems so innocent and so different to the public culture and presence of this normally very staid and self-effacing community. Everybody joins in: elderly rabbis with great white beards and endless shawls draped round them sport rubber parrots on their shoulders. It's simply wonderful.

Travel, any kind of travel, is a constant reminder that there is a self and there is a world and that these are often quite distinct things. At home I blend into the surroundings, they almost constitute me, but on a strange road at dusk in a hired car, or walking from a station to a guest house or around an unknown city centre at night looking for somewhere to eat; all these are reminders of the old dualism that was much stronger in childhood, and in a way only travel or madness restore to the consciousness: the strong disparity between the self and the world. Hence the compulsion to write which in my case these days is only stimulated by having been somewhere new. (As other people only write under the impact of a new love affair, I suppose.) Seeing the world made strange. Or in a favourite expression of mine borrowed from the Swedish writer, Pär Lagerkvist, becoming once again 'a guest of reality'.

* * *

The Ireland trip ended with a visit to Dublin to talk to the people who run the Irish Writers' Centre. I had not been in Dublin for nearly thirty years. My first and only previous visit was made after I had met Larraine in 1965 and we had decided to get married, but I explained to her that I had one outstanding pilgrimage to make before I settled down. I'd always promised myself to go to Dublin to pay respects to the city of Joyce, O'Casey and Behan, particularly Behan who was my hero and who'd died the year before. I'd seen both the original Joan Littlewood productions of *The Hostage* and *The Quare Fellow* at the Theatre Workshop at Stratford East, had read and re-read *Borstal Boy* (which I still regard as a fine novel), and had even stood in the same bar (at Stratford) as your man himself, and caught a beery whiff of his hopeless and self-destructive genius. So I hitch-hiked up to Liverpool caught the night ferry and spent a week in Dublin sleeping on the floor of the flat of some American beatniks I'd met in a bar. They rented a tiny house by the Grand Canal, south of St Stephens Green, full of books, ashtrays, empty bottles and dirty cups. It was the student life I never lived, other than for that week. During the day I read all the books they were raving about; once we walked into town to look at the bullet marks on the Post Office in O'Connell Street, which we touched as if they were revolutionary stigmata.

It was a grand week, with lots of drinking, singing in pubs, folk music, and earnest discussions about Kerouac, Baudelaire, Joyce and Flaubert. One of the things I remember about that week, was that for some reason one of our company when he got drunk always said the same thing: 'as Flaubert said, the novel is a mirror walking down the middle of the road.' We gathered every night in the same bar, O'Donaghue's in Merrion Row, befriended some Irish musicians there, talked excitedly, got very drunk, sang songs very loudly, agreed that our own poems, novels and revolutionary acts would at last turn the world upside down, swore eternal friendship, and assumed we'd live for ever. I never saw any of them again.

This time Dublin looked shabby. Entrances (and therefore first impressions) are of course everything. On my first trip I had arrived by ferry and sailed up the river almost into the city at dawn which was, as all such river-borne arrivals are, deeply memorable; this time I arrived by train at Connolly Station, early in the evening, after a long day's work, and the walk from the station to the hotel seemed yet again like walking through the landscape of my childhood: tenement buildings, very old shops with hardly anything in the windows, broken pavements, and still some horse and carts. I am sentimental about the jaunty trotting of a horse and cart, as my father and grandfather were horse and cart dealers in scrap metal in the East End before the war, and the horses were one of the few things my father talked fondly about in his rare reminiscences of his own youth. But the hotel was wonderful. I'd picked it out of the *Rough Guide to Ireland* which described it thus: 'an old-fashioned, dusty establishment whose downstairs bar is the scene of dedicated, if subdued, drinking by locals.' The room I had was very smart, but the bar lived down to all the right expectations.

The train ride back to Belfast was made on a sunny afternoon. It's a fine ride which takes you all along the coast, along and across a number of expansive mud flats and estuaries, teeming with oyster-catchers and other waders, and then into the green picturesque rolling countryside of Meath, Louth, County Down and the mountains of Mourne.

Back at home I get a phone call from a friend. A mutual acquaintance from long ago called him at two in the morning, 'just to get in touch for old time's sake.' The caller had been going through his phone book, in something of a personal crisis. Two months ago, one Sunday morning, Larraine took a phone call which completely threw her. A middle-aged man in Norfolk called to ask if he could possibly take her out for tea, if she – or her husband – didn't mind. He'd admired her at school but didn't have the courage to say so at the time and he'd never forgotten her. He'd traced Larraine's mother and got our phone number from her under some pretext. She declined gracefully. What makes one, after 35 years, suddenly wish to see someone again? How painful it is at times to open up the past again, in order to attempt to settle some outstanding debts. Or to finally lay some ghosts to rest. My memories of that earlier visit to Dublin had been dormant for years, but just writing those few lines brought everything back, as if I were there again, in O'Donaghue's, waiting for the crowd to come in for another mad evening, sipping a pint, pretentiously putting my copy of *Les Fleurs du Mal*, face down on the pub table. Lighting another Sweet Afton. The future still ahead. But in a way, going back was a way of redeeming the past. 'We are not saints', says Lucky in *Waiting for Godot*, 'but we kept our appointments.'

13 Derry – Moscow August 1993

Northern Ireland now has a grip on me, a hold, a fascination. I like the people, the landscape and the language, and what confirms this affection for me and justifies it, is that the poetry which has come out of Northern Ireland in the last twenty years is probably among the best anywhere in the world – and in such profusion. There are, I would say, more poets of genuine international status in Northern Ireland (population 1.5 million) than there are in the whole of the UK (population 57 million), and it is a phenomenon that exercises me. Why, suddenly, does a cultural renaissance happen in one place rather than another? It can't just be because of the troubles. Plenty of troubles in other places, without this extraordinary outpouring of vibrant words and extraordinary images. The critic Gerald Dawe whose two small collections of essays about contemporary literature and culture, *How's the Poetry Going? Literary Politics and Ireland Today* (1991), and *A Real Life Elsewhere* (1993), both published by the Lagan Press in Belfast, are real treasure-chests of ideas, has argued that: 'We seek to maintain the illusion, at the very least, of being forever of the one place and the one people. This might partially account for the popularity of Irish literature abroad: a consolation for jaded post-modern appetites.' Dawe, much of whose work has been trying to give some wider context to the nature of what he would term 'the Protestant imagination', still sees the role of the writer, of whatever background, as one of encouraging depth and complexity in what is always regarded as a rather simplistic cultural and political debate. As an outsider it seems to me that what many of the poets, novelists and essayists are doing is trying to create a non-sectarian, public space for argument – through poetry, fiction and literary debate. By coincidence the work I have been involved in around public libraries has led me finally, after all these years, to the work of Jürgen Habermas, the German philosopher, whose work on the 'public sphere' is largely rooted in a historical study of English culture and politics in the sixteenth and seventeenth centuries, when the battles against censorship, and for a free press, largely fought by writers, journalists and political critics, created a public realm of ideas at last free of the imposed and dominant views of King and State. This seems to me what is happening now in Ireland: that writers, of both Catholic and Protestant backgrounds, are trying to create a new, non-sectarian public sphere.

The popularity of Irish poetry abroad can't be ascribed to sentimentality, for much of the best work is poetry written in the language of speech – direct, lyrical, passionate, sinuous and committed. It is very northern, too, in that it is about cold winds, difficult terrain, iron age settlements, tough cities with guns and sermons, the affection of small acts of kindness – that is to say it is not anything to do with the warm south, the sun, and the Mediterranean classical tradition – and I've always found myself constantly torn between the two. Have done so for most of my life. At heart I'm protestant, awkward and direct (and too tall); yet I'm also mesmerised by the appeal of sun and sand and warm places, and the languorous writings of the Mediterranean cultures.

There are now two anthologies of Irish poetry I keep beside the bed, and which I've had terrific enjoyment from in the past year: Frank Ormsby's anthology, *Poets from the North of Ireland*, Blackstaff Press, 1990, and *The Younger Irish Poets*, edited by Gerald Dawe, Blackstaff Press, 1985. The only problem with both anthologies is that only one woman is represented in each – the same writer in fact, Medbh McGuckian, whose familial and cultivated images are full of yearning. The great find for me in these anthologies is the poetry of Ciaran Carson – check out his collections *Belfast Confetti*, *The Irish for No*, and *First Language*, tough, vernacular narrative poems which jump start or arc with short-circuited demotic – though I will honestly say that there isn't single poem that I've started reading and skipped in either anthology. Although I try to keep up with the lists from Faber and the others, there is nothing like the constellation of energetic and accessible writing that consistently comes out of Northern Ireland. It's the kind of democratic literary culture I've always yearned for, and I admire it enormously.

Larraine and I flew to Belfast from Luton, hired a car, and were at the Giant's Causeway for tea, having had lunch in London. Within minutes of leaving Belfast airport, you are in some lovely country, pocket handkerchief fields, small villages, pebbledash bungalows, and intermittent rain. The weather we had over those few days was summed up by the sight of a roadsweeper we passed one morning, wearing oilskins and sunglasses. For when the sun does come out, after an hour's rain, the roads and windows of the houses are dazzling. The Giant's Causeway is an extraordinary rock formation of some 37,000 black basalt, perfectly formed, polygons, shooting out of the ground in formation. They are in fact giant crystals. When we visited, there was a thick sea mist, and the coastline was very silent, gloomy and forbidding. The seashore was acrid with the smell of brine, seaweed and broken shells.

We drove on to visit a couple who had invited us to stay in Derry, where the husband is the director of a writer's centre. When we arrived in the torrential rain he told us that this had been 'the wettest May for 50 years', which is like being told in Iceland that it has been 'particularly cold lately', or in the Kalahari Desert that it has recently 'been rather hot'. Despite the sheets of rain which flooded every road, drummed on the roofs of the houses and cars, reducing visibility to a matter of inches, our host insisted that before dinner we should see a bit of the local landscape, and so he drove us up into the hills overlooking Fahan and Lough Swilly and it was indeed quite magical. He then drove us further into the hills, past a modern round Catholic church at the lough's edge where there was a service going on, to another perfectly round building, an ancient castle belonging to one of the many regional kings, itself located on the site of an earlier fort. Looking down through the rain to the loughs and farmlands, the glowing white broken ring of light from the round church appeared unearthly, as if a flying saucer had landed. It was the only non-natural feature in the landscape. Sam told us, as we sat in the steamed up car, soaked and steaming ourselves, stories of the kings of the region, their battles with each other, of the spirits which haunted the hills, rocks and loughs, and though his was a strongly, secular, republican spirit from Derry, still for him the landscape was magical and finally redeeming. I was jealous. I don't have that relationship to a particular landscape.

Such affective ties to place make exile even more painful. In the Glen of Garten, near Letterkenny, is the Flagstone of Loneliness (Leac an Uaignis) on which, legend has it, St Columba slept the night before he sailed from Ireland. Until very recently, I was told, men and women leaving Ireland would make a pilgrimage to the stone, lie on it and pray to St Columba to be protected against the pangs of homesickness.

Back at the house, we had a great meal, with lots of wine, and the talk and laughter flowed, and there was a sense in which politics, social concerns, a love of place, seemed inextricably woven there. Yet the appallingly high rate of unemployment in Derry and Northern Ireland generally is slowly killing generations of extended family networks, mutual support schemes and community identities. Unemployment – and it has to be said defensively, male unemployment particularly – seems to be the acid that single-handedly destroys independent solidarities, and produces a welfarist and dependent culture. That night we slept in the bedroom of one of their three daughters, whose room was covered in posters of – our next door neighbour. For we have a very handsome black young male pop star living next door in one of the housing association flats.

In Derry the centre that Sam runs is largely devoted to story-telling. It is housed in a redundant school, and provides an endless succession of workshops, readings, children's activities, book launches, and so on. Pride of place goes to the 'story-teller's chair', a magnificent, overblown, throne-like, gilt-painted gothic fantasy encrusted with fake jewels designed by a stage set designer, in which it is absolutely essential to sit if you are to tell a story. After a session for children, each child is allowed to sit in the magic chair for a moment. But the fact is that weekly story-telling sessions attract audiences of up to 150 adults, and this revival testifies to the enduring appeal of narrative, and the age-old fascination of a story well told. They get an equal mix of Protestants and Catholics to the centre. Literature in Northern Ireland seems more democratic because the language there seems more democratic – a tough, vernacular, muscular dialect that eschews over-refinement and deracination.

There is refinement in other areas, though, notably the lawns and gardens of the modern detached houses and bungalows that line the quiet roads between towns and villages: lawns trimmed with nail scissors, borders with delphiniums and tulips ranged in line, miniature fir trees in tubs trimmed to the nearest centimetre, not a flower or weed out of place and everything in shocking contrast to the mystical landscape which encloses each garden and is separated by a pristine white chain link fence or castellated low redbrick wall.

We left Derry in pouring rain, with a tip from Sam as to the ideal pub to stay in on the Donegal coast, our next destination. We drove through the gloomy Blue Stack Mountains – about as gloomy as Glencoe, even the memory of which brings on me every time I think about it a fit of depression – and came to Donegal town, the kind of place you mean to stop at but find yourself accelerating out of as soon as you arrive, before a certain kind of angst – brought about by sudden amounts of kitsch – numbs you. The pub in Rossnowlagh is actually off the map, but once you've found it you never want to leave. Just as we reached the coast and began looking, the sun broke through, and having driven past the unmarked lane we wanted twice, we found the pub just in time for a lunch of smoked salmon, salad, home made soda bread and Guinness in a bar overlooking Donegal Bay and the rain clouds lifting off the cliffs and headlands near Killybegs and Carrick.

The sky was blue until 10 at night even in early May, and from our bedroom we could look down on the empty beach in the distance, and the tide coming in as if in slow motion; the breakers seemed to take hours to glide silently glide up the beach, it was quite unsettling. Breakfast was served *from* 9.30 am.

The great thing about Ireland is that the country itself is of human scale. The roads are quiet, you can travel by car, bus or train from one end to the other in a matter of hours. Today I find this more amenable than my earlier slightly frenzied exhilaration to do with the notion of travel and boundless, uncharted space – flying across central Australia with the endless tracts of bleak desert in view for hour after hour somehow seemed more 'authentic' than taking the from bus from Omagh to Coleraine. But now I think I am becoming a miniaturist. Detail is all. I feel relaxed in Ireland, in a way I haven't felt anywhere else for a very long time.

Yet it would take some time to settle, and understand the country from within. As outsiders, unfortunately, most of the names of the towns we drove through or saw sign-posted – Enniskillen, Newry, Warrenpoint, Armagh – are synonymous with terrible bombing outrages or atrocities; yet Enniskillen on a market Thursday in 1993 is a peaceable, friendly small town. My only reservation about the province is that the all the people I've met and talked to in the course of my work there, use the word 'community' even more than Liberal Democrats in Cheltenham, or social workers in Tower Hamlets. I am convinced the word has lost all currency and meaning; it is undefined, open-ended, a catch-all for the very worst of political opportunists, an elastoplast used to cover gaping wounds, and it's prevalence and promiscuous usage in fact cloaks a complete absence of partisan, intellectually informed politics.

* * *

'To return richer in vivid perceptions than in theory....' wrote Walter Benjamin in his Moscow diary of 1926, which is, in my opinion, heresy of heresies, rather a dull read. I went to Moscow earlier this month for five days, and returned with very vivid perceptions, largely caused by being extremely ill with a virus, and hallucinating most of the time. I was invited to speak at a round-table conference organised by the Council of Europe on the subject of popular culture and the influence of American culture on indigenous European high culture traditions. It was felt that the Russians were keen to discuss with other Europeans, whether the arrival of Dallas and Guns'n'Roses meant the end of Dostoyevsky and Glazunov. I travelled with an Italian friend and colleague, Franco Bianchini, via Vienna, the cheapest flight.

We and the other dozen or so European delegates were lodged in the Hotel Ukrainia, one of the seven great Stalinist edifices built in Moscow in the early 1950s to mark out a new plan of the city, and modelled on the Chicago school of skyscrapers from the 1930s. These vast, layered, neo-gothic fantasies rise out of the ground and reach up into the sky like cathedrals – with columned entrances, hammer and sickles mixed with laurel leaf friezes at every stage. Franco and I were on the 27th floor. We got in about five in the evening, having left Stoke Newington at 4.30 in the morning and were tired, but we had been invited to dinner at the Film-Makers' Union building for 9pm, and were offered a walking tour before then. This turned out to be very strange. Rather than walk down into the city centre and pass by some of the more famous sights, we were led by a charming young woman architect for two hours through what was the Moscow equivalent of Beckton Gasworks industrial estate and environs. Every so often we had to cross a 14 lane road – with no markings, mind you – with no central reservation and no traffic lights to disrupt the traffic flow, of mostly rattling, chugging, ancient heavy lorries belching out smoke that covered the whole city in dirt and dust. Near the roads it was actually quite difficult to breathe, as the petrol used by all vehicles is very low grade and gives off a permanent acrid, throat-catching smog to the air. After about an hour and a half we were wilting, as non-descript, barrack like buildings with no distinguishing facia decoration at all were variously pointed out to be the Moscow School of Design, the Institute of Orthodontics, the All-Russian Headquarters of the National Telecommunications Agency and so on.

I quickly came to realise what many people find so threatening about Moscow – that the roads were built on such a vast scale to make the individual pedestrian feel insignificant and terrorised. The city is cut through with badly maintained, pitted and pot-holed concrete motorways; pedestrians have to wait timorously at the traffic lights for the occasional opportunity to cross. In many places there are no traffic lights, and you simply have to run for it. The walkability of a city, I also now realise from my work over the last few years, is directly related to the success of the city as a social space. But where were the people? Moscow on a warm Thursday evening was empty. The streets only occasionally revealed a few pedestrians, people walking dogs, drunks staggering home. On our way home that night, after supper in the club-like atmosphere of the Film-Makers' Union restaurant, where a very percussive pianist and gypsy violinist thrashed Beethoven, Bartok and the Beatles with equal fervour, we discovered where the citizens of Moscow were: underground. The metro system is packed. The stations are built with carved marble, elegant mosaics, Romanesque statuary, bronze reliefs of the Great Patriotic war, genre paintings of sturdy peasants and industrial workers, trains every minute, and the whole system seething with people. They rarely venture up above in the centre of Moscow but gather in their thousands at the metro station and mainline station entrances buying and selling books, kittens and puppies, carrots, bottles of vodka, standing in the puddles holding a bag of squashed plums for sale, selling a single cabbage or sometimes very good-looking grapes, playing cards, children's gingham smocks, anything, just anything.

Back at the Hotel Ukrainia it was suggested we have a drink together before going to our rooms. There was bar on the ground floor of the hotel, blaring out Elton John songs, mostly occupied by young women in miniskirts and young men in suits and sunglasses. Other delegates, but for some reason not me, were pestered with phone calls from prostitutes all night long, or had them banging on their room doors, so much so that Franco had to bribe the 27th floor concierge to stop young women banging on his door. It was depressing, not only the extent of prostitution, but the endemic bribery and corruption that seemed to result from it. Moscow is also full of wrecked cars. The driving is appalling, car crashes all the time. Sometimes people just walk away, either because they are not insured, or because the car is stolen, or because they can't afford to run it anymore. Yet there are also quite a lot of glistening new BMWs, Mercedes, even Porsches, driven around the city by men or women in fur coats, and with the preening arrogance of the very rich.

It's difficult to be positive or optimistic. The Russians we met were intellectuals, middle-aged party members, good liberals some of them, but now driven to deploring the fact that 'the wrong people have now got the money – they haven't been educated to spend it', clinging to the good old days when there was money to make culture even if it came with strings attached. And attitudes towards non-Caucasians that would make you blench. Among the people whose judgement I came to trust, even in such a short time, the gloomiest prognosis was that the Orthodox Church would gain ascendancy, and that by the end of the decade Russia would become a 'muslim-type' state in which the political process was overseen by a more powerful church, to which parliament deferred. Many were dreading the day when Solzhenytsin finally moved back to Russia, because his views are now so messianic and authoritarian that only bad could come of his intervention. Moscow was always intended to be, I once read, the second Rome. I assume that this meant the centre of pan-European Orthodox Christianity.

Communism, I was told by an elegant film-maker at yet another buffet lunch, could only have really taken root in Russia where 'we long for charismatic leaders and authoritarian regimes'. It did seem very strange to me, at last walking in Red Square and around the inside of the Kremlin, to realise that the Bolsheviks had immediately set up their headquarters inside the Czarist fortress, and had buried their leaders – Lenin, Stalin, Brezhnev *et al* – with all the same pomp and mysticism surrounding the dead, next to where the Czars were all buried. Yeltsin has installed himself there now. Surely it would have been more 'revolutionary' to have established a new political district and set of modern institutions in 1917, instead of rushing to sit on the thrones of the dead, to live in their gilded apartments, and to remain fortressed against the people outside. Some delegates to the conference arranged to visit the Lenin mausoleum where you can still see the embalmed body, but apart from the fact that I wasn't feeling so well myself, comrade, I really couldn't cope with what is now patently revolutionary mumbo-jumbo dressed up in red. Unless there is still hope for a revolutionary second coming, when the dead but red will arise and go walkies again.

Franco and I took a couple of hours off on Sunday afternoon and went to the Mayakovsky Museum, opposite the Lubianka headquarters of the Cheka and subsequent secret police organisations. Again, this was central Moscow, but you could count the people above ground on the fingers of one hand. The Mayakovsky museum is perhaps the finest and most radically designed museum I've ever been in, and all afternoon only the two of us were there. It is not advertised, its entrance is hidden behind an office block, there are no lights inside to give the impression that it is open. Extraordinary.

On the last evening, a boat-trip was organised for the delegates, but I made my excuses and stayed in. The traffic, the fumes, the scale of the streets, and the evident corruption were getting to me; I went for a quiet walk on my own for a couple of hours and was in bed by 10pm. But not before spending half an hour in the hotel lobby, sitting and watching the world go by, which was like a scene from a Chicago film. A lot of the men really did walk around with their camel-hair overcoats (it was summer) draped over their shoulders like capes, exuding a whiff of aftershave, and showing a lot of gold round their necks and on their fingers. They were usually accompanied by a girl or girls in the briefest of mini-skirts and at least one or two hench-men, smaller, tougher guys with leather jackets, crocodile skin cowboy boots, scars, tattoos, chain-smoking American cigarettes. They came and went in BMWs or Range Rovers, and you hoped they didn't turn out to be sociologists or professors of linguistics, taking time out. For indeed the conference we attended turned out to have a sponsor – unknown to the organisers – who turned up at the final meal to say a few words and was dressed in a camel coat, a lot of jewellery, with a young woman in a mini-skirt dancing attendance. He said how nice it was to meet all these distinguished people from a happier part of Europe, and that he too was interested in popular culture, and hoped that greater trade links meant greater benefits for all concerned. One of the Russians told us afterwards that the rumour was that he had made a fortune pirating *Emmanuelle* films.

I'm sure I only saw the surface. People who have spent time in Moscow, who have lived there in recent years, tell me that once you get to know them, people are very friendly, idealistic, serious about social problems, and intensely patriotic and religious in spirit. What I saw and registered was filtered through a fever and a headache suppressed by mouthfuls of anagelsics swallowed every couple of hours, but it wasn't very hopeful. Relieved when the conference was over, I became anxious to get home. The bus due to take three of us to the airport failed to turn up. We caught a taxi which ambled along. We got to the airport with 40 minutes to go before take-off (they insisted we be there 90 minutes before take off). We looked for the departures section but couldn't see it. At one end of the huge airport building was a vast crowd, gathered around a single desk which said Customs. We had posh, neat suit-cases and designer luggage. They had TV and Hi-Fi sets wrapped in string and cardboard, motor-bikes wrapped in old newspapers, vast parcels tied up in string, crates of food, egg packing cases filled with clothes, hundreds of people, mostly in families travel-ling to Tashkent or Vladivostock, each waiting to unpack and show their goods to the lonely customs man. At least three hours, this queue, I reckoned. Dazed with aspirin, I said to my companions that there was only one thing to do – to walk briskly and confi-dently right past the queue and the customs officer as if we were staff. We did. Then another queue, with just one checking-in desk for 17 different flights. After 20 minutes Franco nearly brought me to my knees. 'I think they want to see the certificate of customs clearance before they will accept our luggage,' he said. 'I think we will have to go back and start all over again.' Please, please, let this not be true. Sweating we inched our way towards the baggage counter. The plane was now due to leave in 15 minutes. We were looked at with bemusement, then checked in. All that was left was passport control. Franco, pessimistic by temperament, reminded us that it was the passport control people who had issued us with our customs forms when we arrived. Rank with sweat, racked by illness, I could only think of happier times. We were stamped through, and went straight onto the plane with five minutes to spare.

I had not been so ill for years. So in a way I confused Moscow with illness and attenuation, with formlessness and irrationality. Russia became the Other. I regret this, but would have to say that I would only go back if there was a clear purpose for my visit and if I felt very strong and in company. Moscow did for Napoleon and it did for me. Two weeks after, Franco had a fax from one of the Italian delegates. This elderly professor had taken a taxi on his own to the airport. Halfway there the taxi pulled off the main road, stopped in a lay-by and two men hauled him out, took all his luggage, personal belongings and some of his clothes he was wearing, and left him knocked about a bit by the side of the road. Lawlessness is now part of the deal. It is not a happy country, and yet several of the Russians I met insisted on telling me that life was not meant to be happy. There is a resigned air of fatalism, of gloomy national destiny, an unbroken line of tyrants and melancholics, murderous and redemptive by turns, stretching back in the past, and now seemingly into the future. Instant judgements, I'm afraid.

While recuperating from the illness I had in Moscow, I read *The Haunts of the Black Masseur: The Swimmer as Hero,* by Charles Swanson, a history of swimming and the relationship of cultural attitudes toward the body and water. It confirmed me as a certain personality type that feels made whole by immersion and thrashing about in water; I still swim in the local Clissold Baths at least three or four times a week, a sure and certain antidote to tiredness, depression or angst. And there's a lot of that around these days. I read the papers every morning with a tightening feeling in my chest, as the world seems a less and less rational or malleable place, wholly arbitrary, and in the grip of some self-destructive *daemon.* It all seems so different to how I imagined it would be when younger, when I believed that rationality, human agency and the unstoppable force of world socialism would bring everything to heel, in a clean, well-ordered, tolerant and self-respecting comity of nations. While still at school I went out for a few times with a young woman whose father worked at Ford's and was in the Communist Party. She told me one day, in all seriousness, that her Dad didn't think it was worth painting the council house they lived in, because soon the workers were going to take over and everybody would get a new house. And the fruit would drop straight from the trees into our mouths. People across all nations would link hands, and their children would places garlands around each other's necks, and at each other's feet. Then I grew up.

It seems to me now more important to try to bear witness, to describe the world truthfully, and in doing so to understand it. It's an intervention of sorts. I also think it is important to testify to some of the pleasures and felicities of living, which I've been lucky to experience in large measures (I didn't expect that to turn out the way it did either): that in itself may alter the balance of things. Well, it's a risk worth taking. Writers at least seem to have longer epiphanies than photographers. The French photographer Robert Doisneau once wrote that, 'Some days the mere fact of seeing feels like perfect happiness. You feel as if you are floating along. The memory of such moments is my most precious possession, maybe because there have been so few of them. A hundredth of a second here, a hundredth of a second there – even put end to end, they still only add up to one, two, perhaps three seconds, snatched from eternity.' I would like to think that my great moments of happiness could at least be counted in hours, or even days.

14 North Essex – Prague December 1993

A winter landscape. Larraine and I decided to return to the landscape of our childhoods for a reading holiday. We both grew up in Essex, and have mixed feelings about it, but have some fond childhood memories of days, weekends, and even longer, camping and taking caravan holidays around the rivers and coastline. The cottage we have rented is idyllic. Tiny and solitary, it faces south across arable fields and salt-marshes to the River Blackwater, the sky and river changing colour every time you look. At night it is pitch black outside, but that is only after the tractors have ceased ploughing noisily in the dark, by the light of headlamps, snorting monsters, quite disturbing. In the distance, from the bedroom which has a view of the estuary and Mersea Island, you can see the shimmering lights of Bradwell Power Station, like a great square space station that has just landed and from which no-one has yet emerged. It has a kind of ominous beauty and presence in the landscape.

Every morning I cycle to fetch the papers, milk and bread – Peldon, Abberton, Malting Green, Layer de la Haye – about ten miles, cycling a full circle away from the flat landscape of the meadows and saltings of the Blackwater and into the hills that rise up towards Colchester. It takes about an hour. The light is wonderful, grey and cold first thing, but occasionally sunny and brilliant by the end of the ride. The hedges are full of sparrows and tits, full of berries too, rabbits still out on the roads, and even a kestrel sitting on a 'Public Footpath' finger-post looking at me when I stopped to look. On the reservoirs there are wildfowl and waders of all kinds, including cormorants nesting in the trees, which happens nowhere else in the world and is therefore a peculiar Darwinian adaptation unique to Essex. There are lapwings ('the farmer's friend') in the fields along with the seagulls and crows. It is the sky and the light which enthral us. Every so often you can look out and be dazzled by the river as it catches the sun, so bright that you can hardly look at it, and then there are these cascades of light, waterfalls Larraine calls them, which flood through when the sun breaks through a gap in the clouds and streams down on to the fields and the river. We can lay in bed and watch all this through the window.

Because the cottage is so exposed to the open fields to the south, and the coast to the east, it gets the full impact of the prevailing winds. In fact it rattles all the time, sometimes just as a rattle of the doors, but sometimes as real whistles and shrieks through gaps in the windows and door-frames. Our friends Bob and Frances – staying overnight on a visit – approve tremendously. 'It's a good conversion,' says Bob, 'shame about the brickwork above the fireplace though, the only thing that spoils it, stretchers and headers all over the place.' Bob is a carpenter and builder, and I've known him and Frances since we were all in the Young Socialists together, nearly thirty-five years ago. Both of their teenage children have died of muscular dystrophy in recent years, but they nursed them and loved them to the very end, and still appear unbitter and cheerful. Frances still works at the special school which their own children attended before they died. They are devoted bird-watchers, in memory of their youngest son, Carl, who was mad about birds and to whose memory one of the local hides is dedicated. So after lunch we went out to the Abberton reservoir to see some birds.

Essex has some redeeming features and redeeming people – Bob and Frances being foremost among them. The bird sanctuary car park is full of Volvos and Japanese estate cars, the windows of which are plastered with stickers – *Bats Need Friends*; *Adopt a Hedgehog*; *Don't Forget: National Adder Week: March 17–24*; *Essex Naturalist Society* – and the people in the hides, mostly men with grey beards and wearing barbour jackets, have developed a relationship with the feral world that I will never have, and can only observe from afar. (Two days later visiting the beautiful Fingringhoe Nature Reserve on the Colne estuary, I see notices telling me that it is actually National Dormouse Week this week, and inside, among the leaflets, there is one offering a Dormouse Recovery Service).

But we're here to read, and I've started – as part of the weaning process away from London – with Patrick Wright's book about modern Hackney, *Journey Through Ruins*. A lot of my past life flashes up before me as if drowning – life on Dalston Lane in the early 1970s, the De Beauvoir Campaign, the Mapledene Residents Association, the war of attrition fought by the then Labour

Council against all other political, social and voluntary organisations and campaigns in the borough. Labour councils then had an absolutist, siege mentality. The attitude was that if you weren't in the Labour Party, then you didn't exist. *Journey Through the Ruins* is a very good book although Patrick writes in a rather patrician style, lofty in tone (Patrick is in fact even taller than me); yet the writing is saved by the detail and intelligence of the research, and the genuine anger against the free-market that now ravages Hackney as badly as tribal Labourism did before it.

I also came away to continue this writing project – letters, autobiography, I simply don't know what it is – which I feel compelled to write as a witness to the politics of my generation. So I'll tell another story, one I've always wanted to write down but never got round to until very recently, when an investigative feature in *The Guardian* – Ian Katz and Tom Sharratt report on the mysterious finances of a multi-million pound organisation which runs charitable foundations, controversial aid projects, and owns offshore companies and plantations – spread over two days, denounced yet another modern cult, and brought memories back to the surface of the cult I failed to join, or perhaps more surprisingly, refused to have me. It happened like this. I was in the coffee bar at Centerprise (the community centre I had helped set up in Hackney in the early 1970s and where I worked for a number of years) one day, on the lunchtime shift, probably making cauliflower cheese. The light from the front window suddenly dimmed as a huge coach pulled up outside, blocking the sun. It was a foreign coach, a period piece, lovingly restored, and on the roof were strapped at least 30 bicycles. It was full of young people. The coach disgorged and the young people were shepherded off to Ridley Road market – always a bit of local colour for overseas visitors – while a rather serious young man came in on his own and asked for me. His name was Stefan, he said, and he came from Denmark. The coach was part of the travelling high school established by a socialist educational project called Twind. They were travelling in Britain at this moment to 'understand the condition of the British working classes in order to make study materials and to allow the students to meet with typical working class people and understand their concrete conditions.' They were in a hurry. They'd been to Stepney and were on their way to Salford – where he'd heard that the concrete conditions were still not much different than in Engels' time, he said with relish. But he had a proposal. They would very much like a party of typical working class people from Hackney to visit their school and to exchange experiences, 'for only in this way can we understand the concrete conditions of our shared oppression'. A trip to Denmark and the chance to see a real experiment in living, one based on a productive notion of education! I was hooked. If we made the travel arrangements, then they would feed us and look after us for a week.

It wasn't too difficult to find people to go, and the party ended up consisting of a local taxi-driver and his wife, a local teenager with an undeserved reputation for anti-social behaviour (which he later transformed into a fearsome anti-racist, street-fighting reputation), a swimming pool attendant, a home help, a youth worker, a teacher-training lecturer and a couple of others. I borrowed a mini-bus from a local school and off we went. Ten go mad in Jutland. We sang music hall songs most of the way; I shared the driving with one other.

It was agreed beforehand that we would be met in a certain town, in order to make the last 30 kilometres accompanied. Apparently the school was quite difficult to find, despite the flat and apparently empty landscape. At the pre-arranged place at the pre-arranged time, there was yet another of these handsome restored coaches, and there was Stefan with a woman companion, flaxen-haired, youthful, clean-teethed, strong-limbed, smiling: both of them. Here we were, unshaven, coughing, hungover from the night on the ferry, and the addictive smoking. What I remember next is that in greeting us they handed round carrots – like other people hand round cigarettes. Not even washed. You must eat, they are very good for you, we grow them ourselves. Most of us declined. Fucking rabbit food, murmured Tony. Raw carrots, who do they think we are? asked Danny.

Twind proved to be a utopian project in many ways, and I can't bring myself to dismiss it entirely. It was partly funded by the Danish government to develop a new kind of teacher- training. It was founded on the premise that existing teacher training colleges had failed to equip students with a real understanding of those good old 'concrete conditions' which existed for many of the children they had subsequently to teach. This college would be different. To start with, the trainee teachers would have to

ways of these people who watch television and drink and only think of themselves.

Not wanting to make an issue out of it on the first night, we agreed to sing a few rousing folk songs, have a cup of cocoa and go to bed. In fact we met up again in the kitchens after 'lights out' with a bottle of duty free scotch and enjoyed ourselves. On subsequent evenings we had to devise elaborate plans for sneaking down into the village in the dark, not at all unlike scenes from *The Colditz Story* or *The Wooden Horse*: be at the shower block at 8.30 with torches, a quick hour in the pub after scampering across the potato fields, and back for the 10 o'clock discussion or sing song which was arranged for each evening.

Now we could have gone without a drink for a week, but it didn't take long for some of us to realise that there was something not quite right about the set up. There was, for example, a guru, although he wasn't called that but simply described as 'the founder'. Surprisingly he never arranged to meet us although he was on the site at the time. 'He is so busy, he is always working to save the project.' He was spoken of in rather too reverent terms for my liking. We also began to realise that when we talked to many of the students, they always prefaced their remarks with a confession – never a good sign – you know the kind of thing: 'I am so glad to be here, you see, for I was living a terrible life in Copenhagen, drinking, taking drugs and listening to Jimi Hendrix records, my life had no meaning. Now I am helping other people.' Yet they hardly looked cheerful about this. We also learned that sexual relationships between students were frowned upon, and anybody who got pregnant was expelled. There was a clear process of serialisation and atomisation going on. They had thrown a *cordon sanitaire* around the school, and anybody who was inside was saved, and anybody outside was doomed.

To be fair, some of our party enjoyed the week – they were treated with great friendliness, and they enjoyed the many long discussions with the students who treated them, ironically, as complete human beings, whereas the students saw themselves only ever as incomplete, and in a state of becoming rather than being. I hated it. It was puritanical, self-punishing, based on encouraging guilt, arid emotionally, devoid of contradiction, and in every way like a version of *The Invasion of the Body Snatchers* or *The Stepford Wives.* And I know that they found me – nominally the leader – seriously wanting. Stefan told me so. Not good material at all: cynical, worldly, sarcastic, easily swayed by the prospect of a good night out. (In the process of writing this I've thought about why, in some senses, I behaved badly: sullen, rebellious, unco-operative. Then I realised exactly what had happened: Twind had unconsciously reminded me of going back to school – and I had loathed my own school days beyond measure. Unconsciously I had reacted in infantile ways – the equivalent to bunking off, smoking behind the bike sheds, and so on. It was another experience of institutional life which I have endeavoured to avoid all my life since I gave up teaching in the early 1970s. I actually do physically feel ill if I spend too long in a building with corridors and room numbers. My father always said, 'They'll never get me into a factory, I'd rather die.' That sensibility I've come to share, and so too has my brother, who has been a freelance artist all his life. At times it also pre-disposed me towards the American rather than the English novel, where, as someone once said, it is assumed that 'real life happens outdoors'.)

As it turned out, it was a cult. The windmill got built, the network of students and projects expanded, to include in this country a string of charity shops as well as at least one school. But it transpired that there were bank accounts in the Seychelles, mansion houses in Switzerland, and an inner-circle of leaders and gurus who, to put it crudely, cleaned up. *The Guardian* account included interviews with two Oxfam officials who had visited Twind: 'We both began to question whether we had been "brain-washed". We suddenly found that things we accepted with admiration before began to have dubious undertones.' A British ex-student at Twind was quoted as saying: 'The whole work ethic of the Danes there was quite totalitarian, almost fascist.' Another person who had spent an introductory weekend at Twind said, 'Brainwashing is a very fair description of what goes on. With people living in groups so close together seven days a week and isolated from all other social contact, it is a very insular sort of existence: their ideas and beliefs must slowly become identical.' So in retrospect we'd got it right: saved by a pint of lager.

Twenty years later I'm still in some kind of contact with most of the ten who went mad in Jutland – and who proved to be saner than their hosts. Their stories are symptomatic of what has happened in Hackney I feel. Tony works as a labourer, joined

Class War, and when I saw him quite recently at the Hackney Homeless Festival in Clissold Park (organised by anarchists and crusties with military precision and efficiency) thought the Poll-Tax Riot in Trafalgar Square better than Ascot: 'Makes it all worth it, giving the Old Bill a decent lick. Best day out ever, like Christmas and birthdays all rolled into one.' Ron and Doll became religious, and joined an evangelical church. Danny died of a drugs overdose in an abandoned squat and his body wasn't found for several weeks; the home help, Angie, trained to be a youth and community worker and is thriving; the college lecturer I last saw in Charlotte Street, working for a TV company and wearing a suit and flowery tie; and the youth worker, Margaret, had a succession of breakdowns before returning home to New Zealand. (I once spent a whole morning with her trying to dissuade her from telephoning Chairman Mao – she had already tried Nixon without success – convinced that if she could speak to them both she could save the world from nuclear destruction. I'm reminded of her, a smashing person in many ways, if unworldly, every time I play the Little Feat record, *Sailing Shoes*, which contains a track, *A-Political Blues*, of which the opening line is, 'The telephone was ringing/And they said it was Chairman Mao....'.)

* * *

Digressions, associations, threads leading everywhere: life needs a good editor. Back at the cottage we're still following the old routine: early morning cycle ride, breakfast, reading all morning, lunch and then a trip out to another stretch of this remarkable estuary and coastline. Riparian, estuarine, coastal North Essex – it's actually going to be hard to beat we realise. It is beautiful in so many ways, not least of which is a sense of desolation and geographical marginality – even though it is less than fifty miles from London. It is also historically very rich. For example, from where the cottage stands, within ten miles there is St Peters' at Bradwell, a seventh century church on the sea wall which was the third Christian settlement and outpost in Britain after Iona and Holy Island. There is Maldon close by, commemorated in the first poem ever written in Anglo Saxon: the ninth century 'Battle of Maldon'. Less than ten miles north is Colchester, the oldest recorded town in Britain. The bird life is internationally famous, particularly seabirds, ducks of various kinds and waders. Twenty per cent of all the world's brent geese breed in this estuary, and most of them seemed to be on the mudflats at Heybridge Basin when we were there the other day. It was an extraordinary spectacle. We were walking along the seawall when across the river the sky suddenly filled with dense clouds of birds, making a blood-curdling din of quacks and screaming. The sky filled up with these birds as they got nearer and wheeled around for several minutes before all plunging on to the mudflats and coming to rest. The estuary glittered in the sun – the tide was mostly out – and the mudflats were full of dunlins, redshanks, sandpipers and curlews. The noise a curlew makes – a kind of bereft, mournful piping – is quite haunting. On East Mersea, the meadows facing the River Colne are full of skylarks.

For a change of mood one afternoon we drove to the other side of the Colne to Jaywick Sands, which occupies a unique place in English post-war cultural history. It was a seaside resort established by working-class Londoners – 'plotlanders' they were called – who built their own bungalows there after the war. It has been used variously by social commentators of the left and of the right to exemplify either sturdy working class self-activity and anarchist self-organisation, or alternatively, proletarian bad taste and aesthetic mindlessness. It's certainly different. Jaywick Sands is probably one square mile of gridded narrow streets, with a different shape of bungalow literally every seven yards. They all occupy lots no larger than 20 feet by 40 feet. Bungalow after bungalow after bungalow with no space between them, but every one completely different. Everybody designed their own, and the prevailing architectural aesthetic is a mixture of Sunday Night at the London Palladian, Art Deco Essoldo Cinema (North Circular Road circa 1948), Leeds Castle, and Ante-Bellum Colonial Mansion. And that's just one of them. And all on a facade no wider than 18 feet or higher than two-storeys. These are fabulous monsters with bow windows, castellated balconies, turrets and verandas, but now neglected, unpainted and in various stages of dis-repair. The dream has fled. Or rather has turned slightly nasty. It seems now to be poverty by the sea, a last resort for people who have possibly inherited these places but without the wherewithal to maintain them. There's a garish pub called *Never Say Die* and a couple of burger bars, and the impression to an outsider – which is quite possibly totally wrong – is of another experiment that failed.

* * *

Back in London it was a time of small journeys. One was to Ramsgate to catch the ferry to Boulogne for a weekend cycling *randonnée*, early in the morning. I was helped on to the train – into the guard's van – with my bike by a very enthusiastic young man. He couldn't stop talking and was clearly distracted. 'I missed the first train, see, by minutes. I was choked. I'm competing in the UK Triathlon trials in Manchester, but the missus has just gone into labour – it's our first child. So my sponsors have let me come home.' 'It's a big event,' I say supportively, remembering my own nervousness, and Larraine's apprehensions, at the time of the birth of our first child. 'Yeah, nearly 100 competitors, and only three get picked to represent Britain.'

I have also been in Prague, for a European conference on *Culture and Towns* which is now my main area of interest and concern. This is the city that people are predicting will become the 'Paris' of the 1990s, and they could be right. The light-heartedness on the streets, the colours, the cafe life, the bars, the ice-creams, the buskers – it's difficult to believe that less than four years ago this was under the iron hand of Stalinism, a single-party state. I was wholly captivated by it, but that may have been because the company was so wonderful. For I met up with someone I'd always admired – a Scots painter, David, who I met briefly in the 1970s when he was running an arts project on one of the bleaker estates in Edinburgh – and who now does much the same kind of work as I do. We got on very well, as we both did with the crowd of other British, Danish and Italian delegates, all staying at the ghastly monumental Tatra Hotel out in the suburbs, the only saving grace of which was a bar that stayed open until two in the morning. We subsequently travelled as a pack – on trams, buses, the metro system, walking and ambling. We trawled through Prague every night through bars, jazz clubs, restaurants, castles, bridges, and alleys, delighting in the summery weather, the clear night skies and the accessibility of the city to this particular promenading troupe.

Parts of Prague – The Lesser Town and the Old Town – are like scenes from a child's fairy story, cobbled streets, gothic and baroque buildings, alleys, never-ending steps leading almost into the clouds, lights, music, tram bells, church bells, heels ringing on the granite paved streets. One night, we crossed the Charles Bridge into the Lesser Town and climbed the steps to the castle. It's a serious climb. We reached the gates of the castle – which is really a fortified tiny city itself, like the Kremlin, containing the cathedral, the barracks, the royal quarters, chapels, parade grounds and so on, and were surprised to find that we were allowed simply to walk past the sentries on the gate and into the courtyards and squares of the castle itself – the equivalent of being able to walk into Buckingham Palace. Because it was so late there was no-one else around, no soldiers, guards, or anybody. The switch from terror, absolutism and paranoid security to an open society could not be more pronounced. Vaclav Havel was probably in one of those lighted rooms, working, possibly even writing a letter.

I spent an afternoon on my own walking round Josefov, the medieval Jewish ghetto, which has a traumatic history. It is one of the oldest ghettos in Europe – Venice is the oldest I believe – and the cemetery is famous because it was always a walled cemetery and has had to accommodate all the Jewish burials for several centuries, requiring in some places at least 12 bodies buried on top of each other. It is jam-packed, and the headstones lean at all angles, as if the ground were opening up beneath them. There are six synagogues adjoining the cemetery. One of them is a museum of Jewish artefacts, another the home of an exhibition of drawings and paintings by the inhabitants of Terezin (Theresienstadt), a transit camp to which the Prague Jews were sent before going to the concentration camps. A third synagogue is retained as a memorial to all the Czechoslovakian Jews who died in the Second World War, whose names were written on the walls at the end of the 1940s. In the 1950s the Communist government requisitioned this synagogue for storage purposes, and when it was de-requisitioned in the 1980s the names had been painted over – as a 'precaution against damp'. So the slow work of writing again the 77,297 names is in progress, undertaken – when I was there – by two young women students, sitting on scaffolds, neatly hand-painting the names in gold script. As long as names survive – and how difficult it is to erase or abolish a name – then the things and people they represent also survive in some form. For you may remember the story of Lidice – as I do from the early post-war newsreels. Lidice is only 12 miles or so from Prague. In 1942, as an act of retaliation by the occupying Germans for the assassination of Reinhard Heydrich, the village was razed to the ground. All 184 men in the village were rounded up and shot, all 198 women were sent to a concentration camp, and the children were either sent off with their mothers to die or dispersed to German families. This was by way of a lesson – the absolute disappearance of a whole town. Yet when the news got out, many towns throughout the world re-named streets and squares with the name of Lidice, so the original village could never be forgotten. Such is the power of the name, and the naming process.

Memory continues in other ways. There is a well known Czech story about remembering and forgetting, based on a photograph taken in the main square, Starometske Nam, after the war. The brutal and thoroughly unpleasant Communist Party leader Gottwald was addressing the crowd from a balcony. It was snowing, and another party leader, Clementis, lent his fur cap to Gottwald to protect him from the snow. Shortly after Clementis was purged from the Party and hanged, and his image was removed from the official photographs. Except everybody remembered his presence because of the hat perched still on Gottwald's head.

Kafka was born in Josefov, yet it is difficult to equate the gloomy, nightmarish world he inhabited with the sunny and friendly city I and my friends walked around for a few days. I've been reading him again, and it is another world and another sensibility – tiny stories sometimes, of a man who puts on his coat to go out for a walk for an hour, and forgets where he lives. Or of the 'hunger artist' who fasts in public as a circus act for forty days at a time, but who endeavours to fast longer, and in doing so is eventually forgotten in his cage, lying faint beneath the straw until he dies. Yet we have to remember what his friend Max Brod recalled in his memoir of Kafka – that there were evenings when Kafka invited his friends round to listen to him reading, and that Kafka read extracts from the novel which became *The Castle,* with tears of laughter flowing down his face.

On the last night, after the trawl up through Wenceslas Square from the restaurant where we'd eaten an early evening meal – boiled bacon, red cabbage and dumplings that melted in your mouth, washed down with a couple of bottles of beer which we discovered on closer inspection to be 12 per cent alcohol – we went to a jazz club. David, the Scots painter, took us on a detour to re-visit a hotel where he'd stayed with some students ten years previously. He wanted a quick trip down memory lane. The hotel, alas, was in the middle of building works, and this was particularly galling for him because what he really wanted to show us was a basement room which his students had commandeered on their visit as a common room, and which had been decorated with murals as a shrine to Frank Zappa. Zappa is a hero in Czechoslovakia, and at one point it was even suggested that Havel had invited him to become the Cultural Minister of the new republic. Czechoslovakia's most famous band – the Plastic People of the Universe – hounded, beaten up, occasionally imprisoned by the Stalinist authorities – was modelled on Zappa's Mothers of Invention. But Zappa is it seems terminally ill from cancer, and a recent interview I saw with him on television revealed a wasted and exhausted man. I liked him because of his refusal to accept boundaries in music – several years ago Radio 3 broadcast a concert of music by Zappa conducted by Pierre Boulez – and it is good to see the recent re-release of Jean-Luc Ponty's fine Blue Note double album of Zappa's pieces including the delightful *Music for Electric Violin and Low Budget Orchestra, Twenty Small Cigars,* and *Idiot Bastard Son.* But the main point of this digression is that at one point during that detour, David suddenly brought the group to a halt, as we were walking down a street of commercial and official buildings, and got very excited about the quality of the rustication on the buildings. When it became apparent that nobody else knew what he was talking about, he gave a brilliant, impromptu lecture on the philosophy of rustication – which you will now get too. Rustication is an architectural principle that from classical times has informed many public buildings constructed in stone. The first courses of stone-work, usually to the level of the first floor, are laid using stone that has either not been dressed or has been deliberately roughened. From the first floor up all the stone-work is smooth and pristine. This is rustication. The roughened stone represents the rootedness of the building in the earth itself, its rock-like, outcrop nature. The dressed stone above represents refined, polished, transforming culture. Next time you pass a grand stone building, have a look.

On our last evening in Prague we did the town and then went back to the Tatra bar for a final drink. We had enjoyed each other's company enormously. There were a few Germans in the build it themselves and in doing so learn some real practical skills; they would become workers. They would grow their own food, recycle all their waste, build their own boats from which to fish off the Jutland coast, and from time to time travel to Africa to work on farms there, in order to understand the nature of Third World poverty. Nothing really anyone could disagree with. The whole project though was symbolised – just as eerily in *Animal Farm* if I remember rightly – by the building of the largest windmill in Europe which would provide all the energy for the campus, and which as you can imagine was invested with the most extraordinary emotional and symbolic significance. This windmill was to be designed and built by themselves without any recourse to 'bourgeois' engineering expertise. We learned after that they had outlined the scheme to a proper civil engineering firm, which had promptly dismissed the drawings out of hand.

When we got there we were shown into the largest prefab on the site, used as a meeting room, where several dozen smiling young people burst into song, accompanied by guitars and recorders, singing a song specially written for the occasion to welcome the Hackney people to Twind. Then we had something to eat. The problems started. What's this for fuck's sake? Tony and Danny chorused again. Supper was grated carrots, brown bread hewn as if from a stone, thin buttermilk, and an insipid kind of white cheese. And all the water we could drink. Don't worry, we reassured ourselves, a bit of roughing it won't do any harm.

We were then shown to our sleeping quarters, and everybody was split up, even Ron and his wife. Divide and rule. This, it was explained, was so that we could mix in more with them – they being not only trainee teachers but also some pretty wayward youngsters whom, it transpired, the school was being paid very large subsidies by the Danish government to take: young people who had been thrown out of all the state schools and were otherwise 'ineducable'. I shared a double cell with a depressive who couldn't even look me in the eyes. After unpacking and sorting out our beds, we met up again with Stefan. We've had a long journey and everybody fancies a drink, I said, so we thought we'd walk into the village for an hour or so. Stefan's face blackened in an instant. I am sorry this is not possible. It is forbidden to go into the village. It is not allowed. Our community will only work if we live together, and are not distracted by the dissolute and selfish bar, and some Danes. The Spanish barman was keen to close. David noticed a guitar behind the bar – it belonged to the barman, who was persuaded to sing, and very well too. Two songs, and after great imploring, a spirited and evocative version of *La Paloma.* Then it was time to go. But David wanted to sing, just one: *She moved through the fair.* Starting waveringly, only finding an appropriate key in the first few bars, he himself moved from hesitancy and nervousness to full confidence and emotion:

> She stepped away from me
> And she went through the fair,
> And fondly I watched her move here and move there,
> And then she went homeward with one star awake,
> As the swan in the evening moves over the lake

By the end of the song the bar was hushed; not a beer glass was picked up from the bar nor an ashtray shifted. David himself was overcome with emotion even in the singing – it was a kind of valediction. The bar erupted with acclamation; two of the younger women, with tears in their eyes, hugged him. It was the power of genuinely articulated folk song, which can carry all in its thrall. We all shook hands and went to our separate rooms.

15 London – Vienna January 1993

It's that time of year. With spare time over Christmas when nobody else appears to be working, I find myself making arrangements to visit the dentist for a check-up, have another eye-test and order some new glasses. I also go to the doctor as my back gives me more and more trouble as the winter wears on. More fillings, stronger glasses, extra large tubes of pain-relieving muscle gel. Yet all stiffness and clumsiness disappears the minute I get on my bike, or from a sitting position on the edge, topple arms outstretched into the chlorinated and distinctly cloudy and chilly waters of Clissold Baths main pool.

When I went to see the doctor I was literally in the middle of reading David Widgery's book, *Some Lives*! the account he wrote of being a doctor in the East End shortly before he died at the end of last year. All the rhetoric and leftist triumphalism I'd always associated with Widgery in this book is gone. It is a catalogue of despair and defeat. By far the best thing he ever wrote, it's too honest and stark for comfort. Optimistic by nature, there is something about the current conjuncture of economic recession and political disarray that sometimes persuades me we live in terminal times.

As with all texts completely altered and given a new meaning by the author's sudden death, reading *Some Lives!* in the wake of Widgery's own death, there are passages that seem to foreshadow, anticipate – and even long for – resolution and conclusion. I am referring particularly to a section on helping terminally ill patients prepare for their own deaths, which Widgery at one point almost wishfully describes as being the proper ending to lives that have run out of the desire to seek change, and which have grown tired of the intractable struggle to make things better.

Last night I cycled up to a local pub that puts on free-form jazz every Friday. It's an interesting venue. It used to be a very run down Irish pub called the Walford Arms ('the Walford'), near the police station in Stoke Newington High Street of great notoriety. A couple of years ago it was tarted up and re-named Rumours Wine Bar. Happily the clientele stayed put. So its a hybrid place which I think London is good at: a lounge type pub with candles on the table, lots of potted plants in the windows all covered in dust and three-quarters dead, some reproduction Welsh dressers with jugs on them and olde-worlde sign-writing saying things like *Fine Wines & Ports*, and still Bridget and Mike serving pints of Guinness to ageing building workers and the local squatters and crusties. But what is better is that all these different peoples and activities co-exist on occasions like the Friday evening gigs. The Guinness drinkers still stay at the bar, talking over the top of a frenetic whirlwind of drums, bass, tenor and soprano saxes playing discords, glissandos, arpeggios and runs; the punks carry on playing pool, the young blacks sit in another corner chatting and laughing, and around the musicians sit various middle-aged men with grey hair and beards, nodding their heads meaningfully to the music. Half-way through the evening the girlfriend of one of the saxophonists goes round with a cash box and asks, 'Are you here for the music?' If you are, you pay £4 and if you're not, you go back to your drink. It's essentially a trust system, and I like it very much. It is London at its best: tolerant, bemused, casual, democratic. I think a lot has to do with Bridget and Mike who manage and in a sense conduct the pub in a very quiet, well-mannered, easy-going way. They set the tone and everybody falls in. The band, by the way, was the Elton Dean Quartet, made up of Elton Dean (saxes), Paul Dunmall (saxes), Marcio Mattos (bass), Mark Sanders (drums). I've seen Elton Dean on many occasions but this was his best line-up ever and the best gig of his I've heard. He played a blinder, as they tend to say among the *cognoscenti*. The very young drummer was also amazing, and gave the lie to one of the more common jokes about musicians that I think is different in rock music and jazz. What do you call someone who hangs round with musicians? The drummer.

I got talking that evening to a young East German doctor training at the London Hospital and who loves London, particularly music in pubs. He tells me that he spends at least three evenings a week going to gigs of all kinds just to enjoy the atmosphere and the different subcultures. I knew he was German before I started talking to him: what British 23 year old smokes a Meerschaum pipe these days? He comes from near the Baltic, a part of the world with which I am, for no very good reason, obsessed. My favourite collection of poems is called *Baltics*; my favourite islands are the Stockholm archipelago in the Baltic; and I have a very strong desire to visit Konigsberg where Kant lived and died, largely because he never left the town and although the Baltic Sea was only 20 miles away he never saw it. When asked why he had not travelled far, Kant replied, 'I have travelled much in Konigsberg.' Also Günter Grass has a house on Bornholm, another Baltic island, where he does his writing, and *The Tin Drum* was a formative novel for me. Konigsberg is now Kalingrad, and Andreas tells me the Russians destroyed the whole of the old town at the end of the war, and now it is just grim high rise housing blocks and factories. The church remains a burnt out shell but Kant's grave is still there. In my dreams I often find myself in a Swedish or at least a Nordic landscape: lakes, forests, yellow ochre, burnt sienna and green pastel nineteenth century apartment blocks, courtyards and squares; frozen waters; ferries. The air is always very cold and clean. It is not an arcadia or an idyll by any means; but it is obviously obsessive. I never dream of sun, or of mediterranean cultures, although in a way I prefer them. There's obviously something in my character, deeper than my conscious choice, that binds me to that kind of landscape and these strange atavistic images. It is of course no different to the sentiments of Auden in his poem, *In Praise of Limestone*; he also had a thing about 'the moral north'.

Some of these 'Baltic' sentiments surfaced just before Christmas when I was invited to a seminar on 'New European Culture' in Vienna. Representatives from 14 European countries sat in a room in a converted tram depot for four days, discussing the emergence of post-war popular cultures, oppositional cultures, avant-garde artistic movements, and in doing so tried to identify common themes and hopefully forms of support and critical evaluation. It was, as always, fascinating to watch a group of strangers in a very short time meld into a formidably close-knit and uproarious group. There was a buffet on the opening evening, during which people hugged the walls of the freezing and cavernous room, a glass of wine in one hand and a plate of titbits in the other, eyeing each other furiously. Some occasionally swapped formal details of professional backgrounds. 'Oh, the department of social anthropology in Bucharest, well you must know Professor Zlienau, and is he still well?' Three nights later we are all in the Press Bar in downtown Vienna at four in the morning, drinking vodka and conversing at the tops of our voices, a mêlée of jokes, questions, opinions and farewells.

The detail with which many of the Europeans I met there, from both east and west, have lived their cultural lives through the *minutiae* of American and British pop music still astounds me, even though I've observed the pattern for years. The Warsaw sociologist could spend hours in deep conversation with the Spanish Socialist Party cultural under-minister discussing Sheffield thrash bands, missing items from the early Sun catalogue, the changing line-up of James Brown's recorded Apollo performances, or bootleg recordings of Depêche Mode. At times I felt out of it. These people have read the seismograph reading registered by British and American popular music as the most sensitive indices of international cultural change. The break up of Lennon and McCartney was felt in Russia to symbolise the tensions and contradictions in Soviet culture at the time between conviction politics and consumerism. Mroslaw, the Warsaw sociologist, explained in his paper that there are currently three main youth subcultures in Gdansk (quite different in Warsaw or Krakow of course): they are anarchist punks, nationalist skinheads and Depêche Mode fans. They all attack each other. As far as I know, being a Depêche Mode fan in Britain just means buying records: there it is a permanent way of life.

So we talk for three days about subcultures, independent cultures, unofficial cultures, alternative cultures, sozialkultur, autonomous culture, state culture, the 'second culture', working class culture, parallel cultures, oppositional cultures, commercial culture, popular culture, underground culture, socialist culture, and realise that all these definitions at the same time express shades of difference, and that even finding the right words and categories is the main part of the problem. We hear of the Swedish *ragara*, the French *blousons noirs* and *zou zous*, the Polish punks, the Russian teddy boys, the German autonomists, the Italian urban apaches, and realise that every country, east and west, has been characterised in the post-war period by dissident youth cultures, largely centred around styles of music. For the reggae fans in Rumania, 'Babylon' was the Communist Party, and they sang along with illegal local reggae bands about leaving Babylon with all the fervour of Kingston rastafarians. Until punk arrived, said a young woman journalist from Bucharest, nobody had found a way of expressing in songs what we felt about the garbage on the streets, the filthy apartment blocks, the corruption of the *nomen-*

klature, 'punk was the perfect vehicle for our anger and frustration'. The novel seems unable to do this; neither does the film; yet somehow popular music can carry, transfer and modulate feelings and emotions; can represent in one country something quite different in another, and yet still retain its original potency.

Two other cultural movements which had shown a surprising strength in all these countries were, quite differently and quite separately, performance art and mystical religion. I've always regarded the phenomena of 'happenings' and 'performance art' with a bit of an old-fashioned, doctrinaire disapproval. Face painting, taking your clothes off and banging musical instruments doesn't get you very far politically was always my opinion. Yet happenings have played a key role in oppositional movements in Eastern Europe. Painting statues and monuments of tanks pink overnight, joining the May Day Parade ostensibly seriously but deliberately playing out of tune, staging the storming of the winter palace in the streets and coaxing the state police into playing the part of the Tsarist soldiers, giving flowers to soldiers, organising love-ins and free festivals – all this has posed a much greater threat to the system than any number of pamphlets and speeches, because it was done in the public realm as lived symbolism. It is quite affecting to realise how many people, in what was the east, still cleave to the hippy dream: they do want love, peace and freedom. They still do want to party all night. Lennon is still god.

As Hungary began to liberalise, the first major cultural change was the enormous rise in distribution and sale of pornography. Porn magazines and videos were on sale at every street corner, Zolte told us. Yet already that definition of freedom has exhausted itself. The new cultural mood sweeping the country is the human potential movement: transcendental meditation, gestalt, encounter groups, co-counselling and therapy. Why, he tells, us, even socialism is coming back into favour. In Poland the Bhagwan cult has taken off, and a lot of people are into buddhism, mysticism, occult beliefs and astral projection. So the West Coast 1960s is currently being played out east of the Danube and the Elbe. Everybody wanted to know if I knew Dick Hebdige. Just a little, I say. Really! And you live in the same part of London! What does he wear? Who are his favourite bands? In Rumania we all study your Mr Hebdige and find him very interesting.

* * *

Back in Stoke Newington, it's that time of year when there's an expectancy of spring. Larraine and I have been out in the garden, for the first time since the autumn, clearing the dead underbrush, pulling out the sinewy brambles that root at both ends in complex arches and entanglements, dead-heading the geraniums, all the time watched by a pair of robins who always, but always, follow us round the garden as if playing grandmother's footsteps. It's so suburban, if not rural, where we live. Yet just last week a woman was murdered in the next street, as she returned to her home at midday and disturbed a burglar. The following day, because Jewish funerals have to be held within 24 hours of the death, all the streets were blocked as hundreds of the local Hassidic Jews walked from the house to the synagogue (also in the next street). The local paper was full of stories about how this tiny area of Stoke Newington is now overrun with prostitutes, crack addicts and petty crime. Well it is and it isn't. It is a red light district, and the young women walk up and down regularly outside our house, sit on the wall, or hang around the bus stop. Occasionally they even shout out to me as I freewheel onto the pavement arriving home – 'Give us a ride on your bike, Mister!' – and collapse with laughter. They are often pretty drunk, stoned or worse. Yet it is also very peaceable mostly, with the park just a hundred yards away, the handsome churches, the very respectable houses all around, and still quite a lot of pleasantness on the streets between neighbours. It's a strange set of overlays between general calm and respectability with occasional outbreaks of criminality. What knits these two otherwise separate worlds together is the constant rise and fall of police sirens, night and day. The large double-fronted house next door, now converted into five separate flats, was burgled on Christmas Day. Everybody living there had gone away for the day and in some massively opportunistic and successful burglary, all the flats were cleared of every moveable item, including clothes and suitcases. Daytime burglary of the houses is rampant and now, regrettably, murderous. Yet for us Stoke Newington remains heaven. We are sure we could never live anywhere else, and even Ben and Anna have both, on occasions, talked about never wanting to live anywhere but this part of north London.

They've both left home and still neither is more than a quarter of a mile away. I'm always bumping into them in the street, and that is wonderful. Just three days ago I was thrashing like an ageing whale up and down Clissold Pool and noticed Anna in the next lane swimming towards me: sheer coincidence, sheer delight.

Soundtrack

Dagmar Krause	*Tank Battles: The Songs of Hans Eisler,* Antilles ANC 8739
Kronos Quartet	*Steve Reich, Different Trains,* Electra Nonesuch 7559- 79170-2
Billy Jenkins and The Voice of God Collective	*Jazz Cafe Concerts 1 & 2,* VOTP902/903
Miles Davis	*Tutu,* 7599-25490-2
Keith Jarrett	*The Köln Concerts,* ECM 1064
The Triffids	*Born Sandy Devotional,* HOTLP 1023
The Go-Betweens	*Metal & Shells,* PVCC 8942
Smith Quartet	*Kevin Volans, Cover Him with Grass,* Landor CTLCD 111
Ry Cooder and VM Bhattt	*A Meeting by the River,* WLA-CS-29-CD
Balanescu Quartet	*Michael Nyman, String Quartets 1 -3,* ARGO 433 093 2
Gerry Mulligan	*The Age of Steam,* AMLS 63036
Microdisney	*The Clock Comes Down the Stairs,* Rough Trade 85
Artur Rubinstein	*Chopin Nocturnes, Vols 1 and 2,* RCA GK 89836/89837
Various	*Dear Old Erin's Isle,* Nimbus NI 5350
Blekinge Spelmansförbund	*Songs and Dances from Sweden,* EUCD 1108
Hana Dvoráková	*Czech Piano Music,* VA 0010
Kronos Quartet and Astor Piazzolla	*Five Tango Sensations,* Elektra Nonesuch 7559-79254-2
Jean-François Heisser	*Granados: 12 Danzas Espanolas and 6 Escenas Romanticas,* Erato 2292-45803-2